Daily Writing Prompts

Carol Simpson

Good Year Books
Parsippany, New Jersey

Dedication

This book is dedicated to my husband and to my dear Pathways to Literacy *friend, Judy Embry.*

Good Year Books are available for most basic curriculum subjects plus many enrichment areas. For more Good Year Books, contact your local bookseller or educational dealer. For a complete catalog with information about other Good Year Books, please write:

Good Year Books
An imprint of Pearson Learning
299 Jefferson Road
Parsippany, New Jersey 07054-0480
1-800-321-3106
www.pearsonlearning.com

Design and Illustration: Nancy Rudd
Editor: Laura Layton Strom
Editorial Manager: Suzanne Beason
Executive Editor: Judith Adams
Publisher: Rosemary Calicchio

Text © 2000 Carol Simpson.
Illustrations © 2000 Good Year Books.
All Rights Reserved.
Printed in the United States of America.

ISBN 0-673-58895-5
3 4 5 6 7 8 9 - ML - 07 06 05 04 03

Only portions of this book intended for classroom use may be reproduced without permission in writing from the publisher.

Unless otherwise credited, all poetry used in examples is written by the author.

Table of Contents

INTRODUCTION: Purpose of This Book 2

TIPS FOR TEACHING WRITING SKILLS 4

MINI-LESSONS 6
    Capitalization 6
    Ending Marks 10
    Quotation Marks 15
    Descriptive Words 18
    Prepositional Phrases 24
    Run-on Sentences 27
    Parts of Speech 29
    Verb Tense 32
    Opposites and Homophones 36
    Paragraph Writing 41
    Spelling 44
    Assessment 47

DAILY WRITING PROMPTS 51
    All About Me 53
    Celebrations and Seasons 147
    All Kinds of Animals 187
    Fantasy 217

MISCELLANEOUS WRITING PROMPTS 262

BIBLIOGRAPHY OF RECOMMENDED LITERATURE 378

Introduction

Purpose of This Book

Teachers agree that the way to become a better reader is to read. They also know that to become a better writer, one must write. Just as reading needs to be practiced every day, so too should writing be practiced every day. However, many teachers find it difficult to set aside time for writing practice daily. Oftentimes, they don't have a wealth of writing topics at their fingertips. This book is intended to help teachers of children ages 6–10 accomplish that daily writing practice goal. You will find enough writing prompts, in a variety of writing genres, to fill an entire school year. Many of the prompts can be revisited over a period of several days, if desired. Others can be used more than once for a number of different writing projects. Some of the prompts lend themselves to class collections, which can then be bound and thereby "published."

In the beginning section of this book, you will find some suggestions for teaching writing skills. It is important that proper English writing conventions be demonstrated daily. Whether it be the correct use of capital letters and punctuation marks or a lesson on writing prepositional phrases, it is important that children see different and interesting ways to put their words and ideas on paper, while adhering to certain conventions. You will determine which skills to stress, based upon the writings children produce.

In most cases, the daily writing prompts are connected to a poem or trade book. You will find a brief discussion of this trade book or poem along with suggestions for introducing the writing topic. Poems are referenced to the books I found them in. Most references cited are available in libraries and/or bookstores. You may possibly have some of the books on your shelves already. Some of the poems are my own creations and are presented in their entirety.

Once you have begun to use daily writing prompts based upon poems and trade books, you may want to take a look at your own library to see if you can connect a writing topic to some of your favorite titles. It is not difficult to connect a writing prompt to nearly any book or poem. The prompt would come from the discussion that the particular poem or trade book might generate. Sometimes there is a repetitive pattern to the text that you can parody in some way. After using the prompts in this book, I hope that you will create some of your own.

Let the writing begin!

Carol Simpson
Author

Tips for Teaching Writing Skills

In my nearly 30 years of classroom experience with young children, I have found that the teaching of writing skills works better when I base it upon the written work that my students produce. **The weaknesses and strengths that I see in their writing will dictate the direction of my daily mini-lessons.** A mini-lesson might deal with capitalization and punctuation or demonstrate descriptive writing with plenty of adjectives and adverbs. It might be a discussion of how to eliminate some of the lengthy run-on sentences that are typically seen in elementary writing. Sometimes it may lead to a worksheet for additional practice and reinforcement. You will find a few of these types of worksheets included in this section.

Daily mini-lessons are just as the name implies: daily lessons that teach a skill in a short period of time. Mini-lessons are repeated often so that the skills are continually reintroduced and reinforced. I prefer to teach mini-lessons in the morning when the whole group is sitting together, perhaps on the floor, in front of a large sheet of chart paper. There might also be times when I need to pull a small group of children together for a mini-lesson on a specific skill with which they are having difficulty.

Mini-lessons usually cover one basic skill, although other peripheral skills might also be included as incidental lessons. I like to use black or brown markers when copying the writing samples that I use for my lessons and a bright color for corrections and/or improvements. The sentences that I use for my mini-lessons come from children's journal entries, story writing assignments, nonfiction science or social studies reports, and any other written material that demonstrates a particular weakness (or strength) that needs to be highlighted in a mini-lesson. The mini-lesson chart paper is left in view during the day so that children might refer to it at a later time. Chart papers from a variety of mini-lessons might also be placed around the room for reference as needed. They can be attached to pants hangers and then hung from a pocket chart stand, if one is available. Children can select the chart they need, just like selecting something to wear out of a clothes closet!

The kinds of skills that can be taught through the daily mini-lessons are limitless. Children need instruction in the correct use of capital letters, punctuation, verb tense, parts of speech, and other basic English language structures. They also need help in eliminating run-on sentences that seem to plague their writing in the early grades. They need to practice writing what I like to call colorful poetic language. They need to do more descriptive writing so that the words in their stories create images in the minds of their readers. These kinds of skills can be demonstrated, practiced in mini-lessons, and then carried over into children's daily work.

Mini-Lessons

Capitalization

Mini-lessons on capitalization are needed when writing samples show that students do not follow the rules for their use. When doing a mini-lesson on capitalization, demonstrate sentences without capital letters at the beginning. Use sample sentences that contain children's names, days of the week, and other proper nouns, but without the proper capital letters in place. Write the sentences on a large sheet of chart paper and then gather the class (or small group) together. Ask students to help correct the sentences so that everyone sees where capital letters are needed.

You may assign a follow-up worksheet to determine how much information children understand. A similar type of group activity needs to be repeated whenever children's work indicates that a specific capitalization rule is weak. Remember that children probably do not "get it" with just one lesson. Be prepared to repeat it (using different examples each time) as often as necessary! For some children, the skill may not be mastered for another year. Console yourself with the knowledge that the skill was presented on numerous occasions!

The following pages contain some practice passages that need capital letters. Make copies of the pages and then cut them apart on the lines so you will have several practice lessons to reinforce a variety of capitalization rules. Ask children to mark capital letters where needed, circling them or underlining them. Or, you might ask them to cross out the lowercase letters and write the capitals above them. Tell them to use a red crayon or colored pencil to make their corrections.

Look at the work together and correct it as a whole group, explaining what words needed capital letters and why. Collecting the papers and looking over them at another time will show you how much progress they have made. Some children may not need additional worksheet practice, but some might. Once again, it is the children's written work that will determine for you how much concentration is needed on capitalization rules.

Name _____ Date _____

my sister went to disneyland last saturday. she wanted to see mickey mouse. she had fun. some day maybe i can go too.

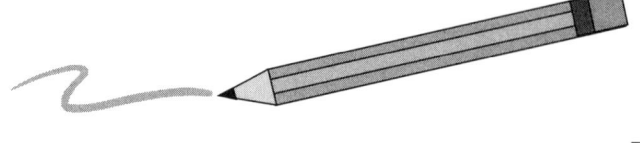

Name _____ Date _____

on wednesday afternoon i had to go see dr. anderson. he is my dentist. he cleans my teeth. he has lots of tools. sometimes i'm scared, but he doesn't hurt me. he is nice.

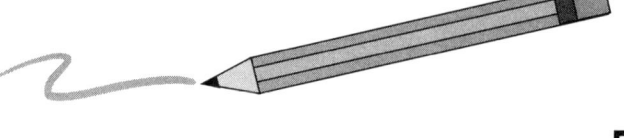

Mini-Lessons: **Capitalization**

Name _____ **Date** _____

my dog rusty is a collie. he is reddish brown. he likes to play ball with me. i got him from uncle arnold last july. rusty is my best friend. we always play outside after school.

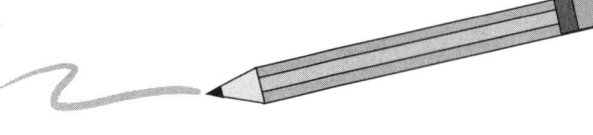

Name _____ **Date** _____

when winter comes i like to play in the snow. i can build a snowman. I like christmas and valentine's day. they happen in the winter.

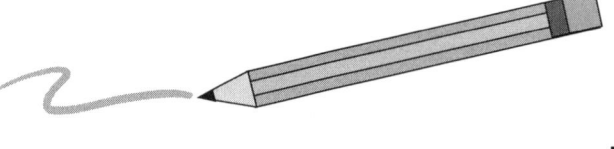

Mini-Lessons: **Capitalization**

Mini-Lessons

Ending Marks

Many children make the mistake of thinking that an ending mark (period, question mark, or exclamation point) needs to be placed at the end of each **line** of text. They often assume that the end of the sentence automatically comes at the end of the line of print. This, of course, is not always the case. In many of the early emergent reading books, each sentence of story text is given its own line of print. Perhaps this is part of the reason why some assume that periods will always come at the ends of lines of print. In any case, locating the correct placement for an ending mark is a difficult skill for some to understand. Choosing which ending mark to use requires an even higher level of thinking.

One effective way to teach the placement of ending marks is to write sentences in different colors whenever the group dictates a story or informational paragraph. Taking one sentence each, from two or three or more children, and then writing each sentence down on chart paper in different marker colors makes each sentence more visible to those who might think that each sentence should stop at the end of the line of print. Verbalize as you write about using all the space on a line, and continue the sentence on the next line whenever necessary. Then go back and have them read their individual sentences from the chart. By adding the new voice to each sentence (as well as the different color), another one of the senses aids in getting information to the brain. They can **see** the sentences in different colors, and they can **hear** the different voices as the sentences are read aloud. And they can see that some of the sentences do not end at the end of a line of print. In fact, most end somewhere in the middle of a line.

Another effective way to get children to proofread for ending marks is to have them share their writing orally. Have small groups gather together and read aloud to each other. The other group members can help the reader place ending marks in their proper places after hearing the text. The reader needs to share the writing at a pace that is slow enough for the small audience to say "Stop" when they think a sentence has come to an end. The reader can then reread the words to see if, in fact, they do make a complete sentence. The group members can then decide what kind of ending mark is needed.

Ask those children who continue to have problems putting in periods to copy short passages from trade books or content area books. Let them copy the sentences in several marker colors, giving a different color to each sentence they copy. After copying, ask children to read the passages aloud. If possible, they could get two or three other readers to help them read the different sentences aloud. Once again they would be **hearing** different voices and **seeing** different colors for different sentences. If practiced often enough, children's work will reflect improvement on this skill. As with capitalization, this skill may not be mastered in one school year. Repeat lessons as often as necessary until most have an understanding of what you expect them to do.

Children who write many words with no apparent punctuation need to read their "stories" aloud and listen for places where sentences seem to end. Sometimes you will need to read the story aloud for them to really hear the places where ending marks are needed. As a rule, if you read the passage slowly and with expression, the children will be able to hear sentence endings. If necessary, pause where the ending marks need to be placed. Check to see if they then put the marks in the right place after hearing the passage read in this manner.

What follows are pages that can be cut apart to make separate practice sheets. Each paragraph needs punctuation. The first page requires only periods. The next page requires periods and question marks. Some sentences might even be given exclamation points. Let children place the punctuation and then ask them to explain their marks. All passages also need to have capital letters placed at the beginnings of the sentences.

Name _____ Date _____

my mother went to the store she bought me a new pair of shoes I like them they help me run fast

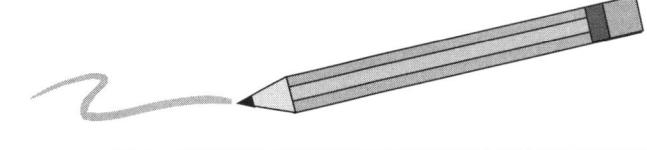

Name _____ Date _____

I went to the zoo it was fun I saw some lions I saw some elephants the elephants were spraying water with their trunks they were big

Name _____ Date _____

I like my dog he is furry he likes to play ball with me I take my dog for walks to the park we have fun there

Mini-Lessons: **Ending Marks**   13

Name _____ **Date** _____

for Christmas I got a new sled it goes down the

hills real fast my sled is red do you have a sled

what color is your sled

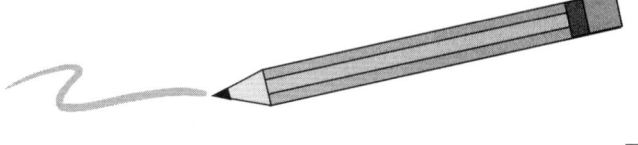

Name _____ **Date** _____

be sure to watch for snakes when you walk in the

forest have you ever seen a snake by your feet

what did you do I saw one once and I screamed

my father came running and scared it away I was

lucky that time

Mini-Lessons

Quotation Marks

Use children's anonymous writing samples to demonstrate how to use quotation marks, as appropriate for the example. A sample that shows an attempt at using quotation marks, but which are incorrectly placed, is perhaps more useful than one in which no quotation marks were found, but were obviously needed. Look for samples such as the following:

Don said I went "to the store to get milk last night."

Ask two children to read the sentence. One child reads the words outside of the quotation marks at the beginning of the sentence, and the other reads the words placed within quotation marks. This should help them determine where the quotation marks should be placed. Hopefully, everyone would realize that Don said more than "to the store to get milk last night." Place a set of quotation marks in the appropriate place and write them in a bright color to show the correction. If appropriate, your mini-lesson could also suggest that they need to place a comma after the word *said*.

For added emphasis and fun, use macaroni to highlight quotation marks in passages. Give children large sheets of paper to write selected passages that require quotation marks. Ask them to glue the macaroni pieces onto the paper in the places where they think quotation marks are needed. This activity adds a tactile approach to learning the lesson.

There is a product on the market that is similar to cellophane tape, but comes in pastel colors. The colorful tape is transparent. Use it to cover text samples in two colors (or more) to show "who said" something and "what" was said. For example, in the following sentence I would cover the words *Billy said* with yellow and the text within the quotation marks in pink.

Billy said, "I have a little black kitten I call Pepper."

Children then read aloud, perhaps by rows or groups, according to the color of tape that covers the words. Use three colors of tape when you are trying to highlight a dialogue between two characters. Readers would then read in three groups: one group as the narrator, and the other two groups as the characters within the quotation marks. This activity helps emphasize that quotation marks highlight what the character said, and nothing else. What follows is a page of short passages that require quotation marks. Cut the page apart on the lines to give students several short worksheets to use at different times.

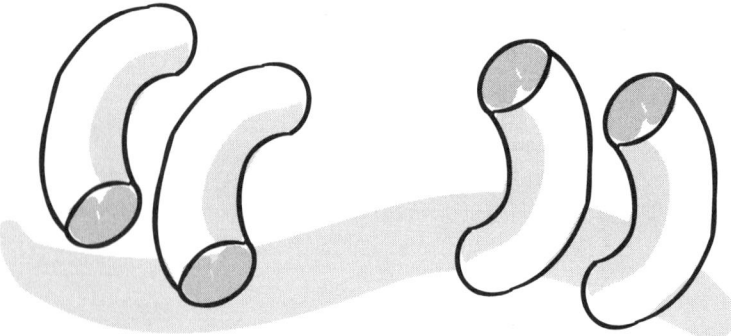

16   Mini-Lessons: **Quotation Marks**

Name _____ **Date** _____

I went to the park said Yolanda.

Blair said I have on a new shirt today.

Where did you put your shoes asked Mother.

Name _____ **Date** _____

It's time for school said Mother.

When will the school bus get here asked Mr. Brown.

Tomorrow it will be hot and dry said the weatherman.

Name _____ **Date** _____

Don't be late for school Grandma shouted.

I don't like spiders and snakes said Maria.

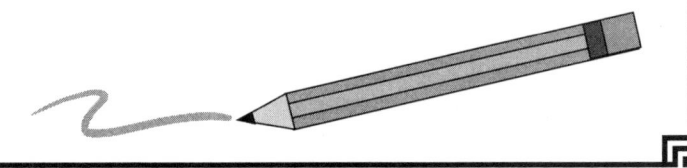

Mini-Lessons: **Quotation Marks** 17

Mini-Lessons

Descriptive Words

As a rule, children do not automatically include colorful language in their writing. They need practice in describing objects and/or experiences using adjectives, adverbs, nouns, and verbs. They need to hear colorful language that grabs an audience and holds attention. Experiences with descriptive language will help children add interest to their writing.

Here is something you might try to heighten your children's awareness of descriptive writing. Ask them to close their eyes and listen as you read Jack Prelutsky's poem "Pumpkin." Now ask them to draw what was described. Words such as *jagged* and *enormous* should help them picture the pumpkin described in the poem. Ask them to recall words from the poem to help describe the jack-o'-lanterns they have drawn. Do they fit the pumpkin that is described in the poem? Read the poem once more and have children judge their own drawings for accuracy.

The first two pages of Eve Bunting's book *Secret Place* contain wonderfully descriptive language. Read these two pages aloud, without sharing the pictures, and then ask children to tell you what they see in their minds. Ask them to draw pictures, if time allows. Children who have not experienced life in a big city will have a better understanding of just how crowded and noisy city life can be after hearing Eve's description.

Another descriptive book is *The Relatives Came*, by Cynthia Rylant. Try sharing this story without revealing the pictures. If children are listening carefully, they should be able to picture the events in the story as they are described by the author. They could then compare the story with their own family reunions. Be sure to share the illustrations in the book after your discussion.

Find descriptive passages in chapter books that will heighten interest in reading the rest of the book. Ask children to select and share descriptive passages from the books they enjoy reading to "sell" the story to other members of the class. Make it a practice to share poetry regularly with children. They not only enjoy the rhythmic words and rhyming patterns, but those who are exposed to poetry every day usually write better descriptive passages because they are more familiar with that use of language. Children enjoy poems that describe, in few words, something they like to do or would like to experience. Dennis Lee's poem "The Muddy Puddle" is fun to read because of the way the words flow off your tongue as you say them. Children laugh at the vision of someone sitting in a muddy puddle and imagine how it must feel. They want to hear the words over and over again. It is fun to talk about the way mud feels and what the children want to do when they see mud puddles. To take this further, cut a piece of tagboard in the shape of a puddle and fill it with words that describe the puddle and how it feels. You could also share the poem "Mud," by Polly Chase Boyden. Talk about how mud feels (or might feel) between their toes. The words the children name to tell about how mud feels are descriptive indeed! The follow-up stories they often write are quite funny!

A good way to help children practice descriptive writing is by having them tell how something looks, feels, tastes, smells, and sounds. Ask them to describe a picture they have drawn themselves, or one you provide. The picture might be of a colorful garden or an undersea view of a coral reef, for example. The more colorful the picture, the better. Have them describe what they see, feel, taste, smell, and hear based upon the picture. Tell them to use "colorful language" in their descriptions. You might be surprised at the results.

Lucie Hymes has written a poem called "Beans, Beans, Beans" that contains many adjectives. It's a great example of just how descriptive adjectives can be! Ask students to use the basic rhyming pattern of this work to write their own adjective-filled poem about books, shoes, pies, and so on. To reveal the basic pattern of the poem, remove all of the adjectives, change the "beans" words to your new topic as suggested earlier, and maintain the few words that guarantee rhyme in the poem. Third-graders enjoy writing their own versions of this poem independently. First- and second-graders need a little more help, but can succeed with prompting.

The following pages contain blank spaces for students to write words that describe a variety of things. Remind them to think about using words in their writing that tell what they see, feel, taste, smell, and hear.

Name _____ **Date** _____

Use your senses when you describe the following.

An apple tree _____
_____
_____

A plate of spaghetti _____
_____
_____

A busy street _____
_____
_____

Name _____ **Date** _____

A rabbit has:	**A frog has:**
a _____ body	a _____ body
two _____ eyes	two _____ eyes
_____ legs	_____ legs
a _____ nose	a _____ nose

A flower is _____, _____, _____, and _____.

A car is _____, _____, _____, and _____.

My school is _____, _____, _____, and _____.

Mini-Lessons: **Descriptive Words** 21

Name _____ **Date** _____

Think of words that describe yourself, using the letters of your name. Use the examples below to help you.

K - kind
E - energetic
N - noisy
D - dainty
R - runner
A - alive

J - jumpy
U - unusual
N - neat
I - independent
O - old
R - reader

Now try it below, using your own name.

_____ - _____
_____ - _____
_____ - _____
_____ - _____
_____ - _____
_____ - _____
_____ - _____
_____ - _____
_____ - _____

Mini-Lessons: **Descriptive Words**

Name_____ Date_____

Add adjectives and adverbs in the blank spaces to make the sentences more interesting.

Horses run.

_____ horses run.

_____ horses run _____.

Lions roar.

_____ lions roar.

_____ lions roar _____.

Children play.

_____ children play.

_____ children play _____.

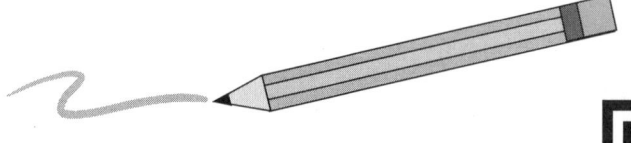

Mini-Lessons: **Descriptive Words**

Mini-Lessons

Prepositional Phrases

Prepositional phrases can add a lot of information to a story. Have children practice prepositions by adding phrases that tell "where" to sentences that they write. The book *Rosie's Walk,* by Pat Hutchins, tells about Rosie the hen and her journey around the barnyard. Share the book and then make a list of the numerous prepositional phrases that tell where Rosie went. Follow this activity with a discussion of another animal, such as a mouse, and where it might hide in your house if you were trying to catch it. Give children a sheet of drawing paper with the following sentence starter to copy and complete.

The mouse went_____.

Children need to tell where the mouse went and then illustrate their sentence.

If they are told to use at least three words to tell "where," they will be less apt to say that "the mouse went home." Children might choose to write that "The mouse went . . . behind the door" or " . . . under the bed" or " . . .out the window."

Ask children to write other prepositional phrases that tell "when." Supply paper and have them write the following sentence.

I like to read books _____.

Have children complete the sentence telling "when" (i.e., after lunch, before recess, at bedtime, etc.). Then, if you wish, they could draw an accompanying picture. Reiterate that prepositional phrases help to make writing more interesting to the reader. When you find good examples in your children's work, highlight those examples by sharing them with the whole class. You need not tell who wrote them. Copy the sentences on chart paper and let the class know that this is the kind of writing you like to see.

Eleanor Farjeon's poem "Cats" contains many prepositional phrases that tell where cats sleep. By showing prepositional phrases as they appear in context, you will help children understand how they might improve their own writing by telling **where** and **when** events happen.

Another example of prepositions in context is the poem "Thanksgiving Day," by Lydia Maria Child. Have children listen and then recall all of the places where the horse takes the sleigh on the way to Grandfather's house.

Name _____ **Date** _____

Finish the phrases that tell *where* the mouse went.

The mouse went *under* _____.

The mouse went *over* _____.

The mouse went *through* _____.

The mouse went *by* _____.

The mouse went *in* _____.

The mouse went *up* _____.

The mouse went *down* _____.

Name _____ **Date** _____

Finish the phrases that tell you *when* you like to read.

I like to read *before* _____.

I like to read *after* _____.

I like to read *at* _____.

I like to read *until* _____.

I like to read *during* _____.

Mini-Lessons: **Prepositional Phrases**

Mini-Lessons

Run-on Sentences

A common problem with stories written by primary children is the run-on sentence. Some write and write until they fill a whole page with one sentence by adding the word *and* or the phrase *and then* . . . over and over again. One way to help alleviate this problem is to ask writers to read their text as it is written and not take a breath until they come to a period or other ending mark. They will understand and appreciate the problem of run-on sentences as they run out of breath! Now ask them to circle all of the . . . *and then* . . . phrases (or the word *and*). Then have them reread the text aloud to a peer (or to you) and omit the circled parts. The listener should check to see whether the text makes sense without the phrases. The reader should realize that it is much easier to read a complete sentence without running out of breath when the sentence is of a more reasonable length.

Once again, write sentence examples in a variety of marker colors. If children see a run-on sentence written in a single color, and filling many lines on a piece of paper, they may more easily realize that the sentence is too long. Use different colors to write several sentences rather than just one very lengthy one. Then compare the two examples and discuss which one sounds better and is easier to read.

The following page contains some examples of run-on sentences. Copy the page and cut it apart, if desired. Ask students to read the run-on sentences and then circle the . . . *and then* . . . phrases. Read the sentences once more, omitting the . . . *and then* . . . parts. Which sentence sounds better? Are there other words that might sound more interesting in place of . . . *and then* . . . ?

Name _____ Date _____

My mom said I could go to the park and then I called my friend and then we went to the park and played baseball and then we invited some other kids to come too and then we had to go home and eat.

Name _____ Date _____

I like to make pizza. First I make the crust and then I put on some pepperoni and then I put on some sauce and then I put on some cheese and I put the pizza in the oven and when it's done I eat it.

Name _____ Date _____

A caterpillar comes out of an egg and it starts to eat and eat lots of leaves and when it gets full it makes a cocoon and it curls up inside and when it is ready it comes out and it is a butterfly or moth and it flies away.

Mini-Lessons: **Run-on Sentences**

Mini-Lessons

Parts of Speech

Children in the elementary grades usually understand basic parts of speech (nouns, verbs, and adjectives) if they are presented in context and if they are explained in simple terms. Poetry works well as a sample because it very often describes a scene or event in just a few lines or sentences.

Select a short poem and write it on chart paper. Ask children to find the nouns, verbs, and adjectives. As they name them, underline them with a variety of marker colors using, for example, red for nouns, blue for verbs, and green for adjectives. Explain the concept of a noun as "a word that names something you can draw." Although not all nouns can be explained in terms that simple, for this age group, it is a sufficient explanation of what a noun is. As children gain confidence, they will enjoy searching for nouns in the poems and story passages.

To study verbs, tell children that "a verb tells something your body can do." Add that you usually can add *-ing* to a verb. Again, this is a very simple explanation and will not lead to the discovery of all verbs, but it makes verbs much easier for children to understand. When underlining the verbs in a poem or story passage, ask children to name a verb and then say their word once more by thinking "I can ____." The poem "Jump or Jiggle," by Evelyn Beyer, is an excellent example of verbs in context.

Adjectives are described as those words that tell us more about nouns. If you share Jack Prelutsky's "Pumpkin" poem, children will be looking for those words that tell more about the way the pumpkin looks. Rose Fyleman uses several descriptive words in her poem "Mice." Children will discover that words that name colors are usually adjectives.

Although children who understand adjectives could also understand adverbs, they are usually not taught at this level. If you wish to introduce them, you might have children name adverbs when given a poem or story where they are asked to name "descriptive words." Accept their answers and then talk about how their descriptive words tell more about how something is moving.

Name _____ Date _____

Circle nouns in red. Circle verbs in blue.
Circle words that describe in green.

1. Whales swim quickly in the sea.

2. The bus raced down the street.

3. My little sister writes funny words.

4. A yellow banana tastes yummy.

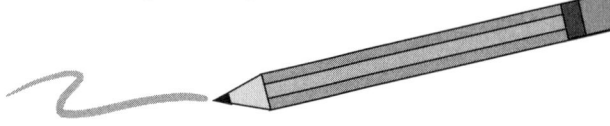

Name _____ Date _____

Find the nouns, verbs, and describing words.

"My Snowman"

My snowman wears a big black hat.

A carrot is his nose.

The scarf of red around his neck

Feels warm in winter snows.

The sun comes out and warms the day.

My snowman gives a holler.

He does not think he'll last long now.

He keeps on getting smaller.

Mini-Lessons

Verb Tense

In the English language there are various ways of changing the tense of a verb so that it matches the meaning of the rest of the sentence. Adding the traditional *-ed* ending doesn't create a past tense verb in all cases, just as adding *-ing* doesn't always make a verb show present tense. Many times writers must go with what "sounds right" because of odd verbs. You can have children practice changing verbs from present to past tense but unless it is shown in context, the exercise will probably not result in much understanding of the concept.

Have children work on question/answer relationships and verb tense at the same time by answering questions about a familiar story or poem. The example on the next page contains questions about *The Three Little Pigs*. Tell children to reconfigure the words in the question when writing their answers. Practice this kind of question/answer strategy verbally, giving many examples before expecting children to consistently use the skill.

On the second page are questions that can be answered using the poem "Wendy in Winter," by Kaye Starbird. This poem is excellent for teaching cause and effect: Wendy has all sorts of problems because of her actions.

The third page contains a selection of double sentences. The verb in the first sentence is written in the present tense. It needs to be highlighted and discussed. Children are asked to complete the related sentence by filling in the verb in its past tense form. You may want to do examples of regular verbs and irregular verbs prior to doing the worksheet. There are examples of both kinds in the lesson.

Name _____ Date _____

Be sure to use words from the question to write your answers. (Example: Why did the wolf knock on the door? Answer: The wolf knocked on the door because . . . .)

1. Why did the three pigs build new homes?

_____
_____
_____

2. Why did the wolf blow on the pigs' houses?

_____
_____
_____

3. Why did the third little pig put a pot of hot water in the fireplace?

_____
_____
_____

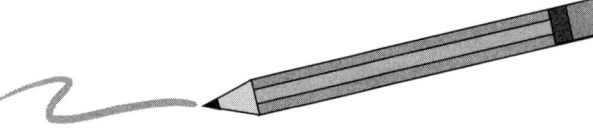

Mini-Lessons: **Verb Tense**   33

Name _____   Date _____

Questions come from the poem "Wendy in Winter" by Kaye Starbird.

Remember to use words from the question to write your answers. (Example: Why did the apple bough sag? Answer: The apple bough sagged because . . .)

1. Why did Wendy's coat blow off?

_____
_____
_____

2. Why were Wendy's feet frozen?

_____
_____
_____

3. Why does Wendy have stitches?

_____
_____
_____

Mini-Lessons: **Verb Tense**

Name_____ Date_____

Practice changing verb tense from present to past.

I am running. Yesterday I _____.

I am making soup. Yesterday I _____soup.

I am helping my mom. Yesterday I_____her.

I am eating pizza. Yesterday I_____spaghetti.

I have a new puppy. Yesterday I _____a cat.

I can win the race. Yesterday I _____a prize.

I give you money. Yesterday I _____you none.

I turn on the water. Yesterday I _____it off.

I am playing ball. Yesterday I _____soccer.

I swim in the pool. Yesterday I_____in the lake.

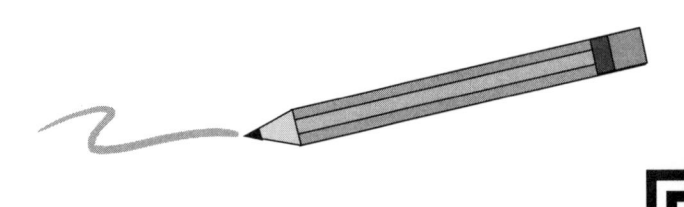

Mini-Lessons: **Verb Tense**　35

Mini-Lessons

Opposites and Homophones

Children need practice working with different of kinds of words in their writing. Practice helps them gain confidence in writing longer and more descriptive sentences and paragraphs. What follows is a selection of reproducible pages that ask children to consider words that are opposites and words that are homophones.

If you have the space, either on a wall or chart stand, it is a good idea to make, and keep handy, lists of special words such as homophones, opposites, and common rhyming families. If children have access to these lists, they may try to check their own writing to make sure they have used the correct word and spelling. Brainstorming with children is a good way to create these lists. They are more apt to use the words as a resource if they have had a hand in creating them.

In the "Miscellaneous Writing Prompts" section, p. 308, you will find directions for making reversible books. Use this type of writing project to check knowledge of opposite words.

Name _____   Date _____

Write words that are the opposite of the words listed.

fast _____   hot   _____

quiet _____   brave _____

tough _____   tame _____

old   _____   tall _____

dark _____   mean _____

happy _____   soft _____

high _____   good _____

off   _____   out   _____

yes   _____   down _____

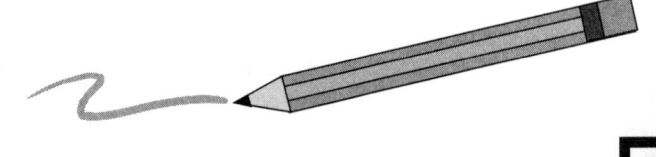

Mini-Lessons: **Opposites and Homophones**

Name_____ Date_____

Can you find the pairs of opposites in this poem?
List them together on the lines at the bottom of the page.

Li'l Red and the Wolf

That <u>mean</u> <u>old</u> wolf who fooled Li'l Red

Was not very <u>nice</u>, I've heard it said.

<u>His</u> teeth were <u>big</u> and his heart was <u>small</u>.

He had no concern for <u>young</u> Red at all.

In the blink of an eye he was in Granny's bed

With blankets that covered him <u>up</u> to his head.

Like a <u>good</u> girl would, Li'l Red came <u>in</u>

When that <u>bad</u> wolf cried <u>out</u> with a grin,

"Come closer my sweet, I just want to see you."

But when <u>she</u> looked <u>down</u> he said, "I'm going to eat you!"

It was lucky for all that a hunter was near.

<u>He</u> saved Li'l Red and <u>her</u> kind granny dear.

Name _____ Date _____

Which word fits correctly in each blank?
Write it on the line.

1. I walked _____ the store and got _____ cookies. Would you like one _____?

| two | to | too |

2. Did you _____ that there are _____ animals on the moon?

| no | know |

3. _____ is a dog in _____ backyard and _____ not afraid of it.

| their | they're | there |

4. I can _____ the birds sitting _____ in the tree.

| here | hear |

5. I will _____ a book written _____ my favorite author.

| by | buy |

Mini-Lessons: **Opposites and Homophones**   39

Name_____ Date _____

Find and underline the pairs of homophones.

When I hear a bird singing, I know that spring is here. The birds are building their nests in the tall trees. There is no more snow on the ground. Mother bear will come out of her cave where she and her cub have hibernated. The stories I write are about playing outside on a warm day. A light jacket is the right thing to wear to school. When I wear shorts my legs are bare. A winter coat is too heavy now. Yesterday I read a book about things to do in spring. The wind blew my red and blue kite when I tried to fly it. I need to buy a new one. I saw storm clouds passing by.

Mini-Lessons

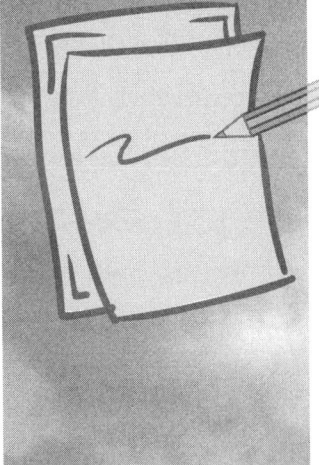

Paragraph Writing

Model putting sentences together in paragraph form when discussing a single topic. For demonstration purposes, use the story on p. 43. Tell children that this is a story about cats. The cat family contains many animals that have some common characteristics, yet each type of cat has its own identity. A story about cats might contain an opening paragraph about the cat family and then several paragraphs about types of cats, followed by a closing summary paragraph. Have them divide the story into paragraphs. Paragraph breaks should be marked after *alike, animals, tail,* and *jungle.*

The cat story example is only one of many ways to demonstrate writing stories with different paragraph topics. Another example might be to write about the members of a household. The commonality is that the people all share the same dwelling. But each individual has his or her own name, characteristics, and personality. Each person gets a separate paragraph.

Ask children to write a story about three different times in their lives. For example, the first paragraph tells about their life as a baby; the second paragraph tells about their first day of school; and the final paragraph tells about their life now, including their current age and grade in school. The common thread that holds the story together is that it is all about one person.

To further illustrate the connection between stories and paragraphs, draw an outline of a house. Explain that this represents the general subject of the story. As rooms are sketched into the house outline, explain that each room tells about part of the subject of the story. Each room takes up its own space in the house just as each paragraph takes up its own space in the story. Just as the refrigerator would not belong in a bedroom, a sentence about a snowman would probably not belong in a paragraph about swimming.

Name _____ Date _____

Divide the following story into paragraphs by drawing a slash (/).

There are many members of the cat family. All cats have four legs, whiskers, and paws with claws. But not all cats look alike. A lion is a big yellow cat. Its tail has a tuft of fur on the end. The male lion has a large mane around its head. Lions catch and eat other animals. Cheetahs are fast. They are the fastest land animal. They have black spots on their fur coats. A cheetah has a small head and long tail. The cat that lives in the house next door is small. It has stripes like a tiger, but it is not dangerous. It lives in a house, not in the jungle. Cats are beautiful, graceful animals. They are fun to watch, but they are not all fun to play with. Look for other members of the cat family at the zoo.

Mini-Lessons: **Paragraph Writing** 43

Mini-Lessons

Spelling

Spelling becomes an issue when we ask children to put pencil to paper and produce a piece of writing. We want children to succeed in learning spelling words, but we are sometimes afraid that the desire for perfect spelling could hamper creative thoughts and ideas. There are children who are so anxious about spelling that their writing contains only words they know they can spell. Their creative thoughts become stifled and plain. Then there is the opposite situation, namely, the child who cares nothing about spelling and so will write words quickly without regard for whether they are spelled correctly. We need to teach to both of these children's needs.

One way to try to improve spelling is to create a Word Wall Chart. A Word Wall takes a sizable amount of space, but if it is being used, it is worth it. The typical word wall contains basic sight vocabulary words that form the major portion of our oral and written language. They are written in large enough print so that they can be seen easily by everyone. Words fit nicely on 4" x 6" file cards. Use dark broad tip permanent markers when writing the words so as to prevent fading. If more space is needed, the word cards can be cut down to the shape of the words written on them. Two-letter words, for example, take up less space if they are cut to shape rather than mounted on the full 4" x 6" card. If the words are arranged or grouped in alphabetical order, the task of finding a specific one becomes much easier. Encourage children to refer to the Word Wall when doing their written work. When they misspell words from the Word Wall, circle the word or words and write a W/W beside them to indicate that the words were on the word wall. If students see enough circled W/W words on their papers, they will begin to refer to the wall more often and improve their spelling habits and skills.

Another useful wall chart is a Brainstorming Chart. On it are special words that might be important in the writing of a specific story idea but that are difficult to spell. Keep in mind that the brainstorming words are not the ones to be found on the Word Wall, but are special words children would probably not be able to spell without help. Some children would otherwise not use these words in their stories for fear of misspelling them. By creating and displaying the Brainstorming Chart first, you are leveling the playing field prior to the actual writing. Expect all children to correctly spell the words on the Brainstorming Chart in their assignments.

After students complete the special writing assignment, hang the Brainstorming Chart by a pants hanger on a metal chart stand for future reference. The words might also be written on the pages of a teacher-made class dictionary. This dictionary contains all of the words that are put on Brainstorming Charts during the course of the school year. Put the words in the class dictionary as each Brainstorming Chart is put away. The class dictionary is placed in a convenient location for use by all children.

A variation on the idea of the class dictionary is to hang 26 individual letter pages on a large wall space or to the bottom of the chalkboard ledge. Pages are made using file folders cut to 8" x 10-1/2" size. *If you cut them the traditional 8" x 11" size, they do not easily slide in and out of the sheet protectors in which they will be placed.* Words from Brainstorming Charts are written on these pages. It helps students find particular words if you number them as you write them on the 8" x 10-1/2" cards. The letter pages are placed inside plastic sheet protectors with an open top, one letter page per sheet protector. The sheet protectors also have holes punched on the left side for placing them in 3-ring binders. If wall space is not available, put the pages of your class dictionary together with metal rings or place in a binder. When a child needs help spelling a word, he or she could pull out the page needed and leave the rest of the dictionary pages in place.

Cut apart an alphabet chart that contains letters and corresponding sound pictures. Tape a letter (you may want to use both capital and lowercase) and the corresponding sound picture to the *front* of each plastic sheet protector. This helps children quickly identify the page they need when looking for a specific word. If they cannot figure out which letter they need, they can refer to the picture. Example: A student might think "The word I want to spell starts with the same sound as the picture of the fish. Maybe I'll find my word on that card."

Mini-Lessons

Assessment

Use the following assessment form to help you measure what students are and are not doing when they write. This assessment works well for specific writing assignments; you would not want to use it for evaluating journal entries or impromptu writing. Grade-four children can use the form as a self-assessment tool by comparing their scores to the ones you gave and discussing differences. Younger children should not use the form for self-assessment; however, they should be given an explanation of what is going to be expected of them in their written work. Show them the assessment form and explain each part carefully, as it applies to the individual writing assignment. Looking at their assessment sheet will show children where they need to improve.

Each item to be assessed is given 1, 2, or 3 points, 3 points being the best. Note the descriptions of the number values at the bottom of the assessment sheet. A total score of less than 8 out of 15 possible points (below 50%), indicates that a child needs to concentrate on specific writing skills.

The first criterion, "Followed directions given," assumes that some specific directions are given prior to the writing assignment. Assign a point value of 3, 2, or 1 based upon the child's ability to comply.

"Used appropriate capitalization" and "Used appropriate punctuation" are both self-explanatory. The skills are either being consistently applied, progress is being made, or the child needs more work on it.

Mini-Lessons: **Assessment** 47

"Story or narrative makes sense" indicates that the work is understandable and that it follows a natural sequence. Someone reading the work would not wonder what the child was trying to say.

"Sentences are complete and do not ramble" indicates that the student has looked for and eliminated any run-on sentences or fragments. Careful reading, perhaps aloud to a peer, will help him or her locate any of these problems.

The assessment sheet is simple to use. It does not cover every aspect of children's writing, but it is also easy for students to understand and easily presented and explained to parents at conference time.

Assessment Sheet

Name _____ **Date** _____

Project /title _____

_____ Followed directions given

_____ Used appropriate capitalization

_____ Used appropriate punctuation

_____ Story or narrative makes sense

_____ Sentences are complete and do not ramble

_____ Total points earned out of 15

3 = consistently applied   2 = showing progress   1 = needs some work

TOTAL POINTS   13–15 points = 3 (skills are consistently applied)
                8–12 points   = 2 (student is making progress)
                0–7 points   = 1 (student needs more work)

Daily Writing Prompts

What follows is a collection of writing prompts. Some will lead to stories while others will lead to lists, letters, postcards, and other types of writing. Some will result in works of fiction while others will lead to nonfiction writing. Children need to write daily and with a variety of purposes in mind. Some prompts will result in persuasive writing while others will lead to expository or narrative writing. The main focus of this section of the book is to help you engage children in writing every day.

The writing prompts are arranged in categories to help you organize them. They are not meant to be used in sequence and do not increase in difficulty. Pick and choose subjects as they are needed and will fit into your classroom schedule. Although most prompts lead to individual "stories," there are some that can result in class collections or class books, if desired.

Whenever possible, the writing prompts are linked to books or poems. Although it is helpful to share the book or poem before putting pencil to paper, it is not a necessity, except in very few instances. The book or poem is meant to lead to a discussion of a topic before the writing takes place. It is possible to initiate the suggested discussion without the use of the book or poem. In a few cases the book or poem is necessary in order to follow a pattern or add text to a story that has something missing.

Two books were used as references for most of the poems you will find listed. Those two books are *The Random House Book of Poetry for Children,* with poems selected by Jack Prelutsky, and *Poetry Place Anthology,* published by Scholastic/Instructor Books. The poems that are present on the teacher page are written by the author. They have been shared with children over the years and have been found to be useful in initiating discussions about various subjects.

For your convenience, there is a bibliography at the end of the book that gives citations for each book recommended.

All About Me

The writing prompts that follow are reflective of personal experiences, feelings, and ideas. All are written from the child's own point of view. Subject matter includes family and friends, favorite books, personal feelings and problems, to name but a few.

Don't forget to help the writing process by putting up Brainstorming Charts when needed (see p. 45). Words that name family members and relatives are often used with these prompts. Often you will find that allowing children to draw a picture to go with their stories augments their writing experience. Sometimes the picture will need to come first and the writing will follow and will describe what has been drawn.

Quick! Get Me a Bandage!

Shel Silverstein's "Band-Aid" poem, which can be found in his book *Where the Sidewalk Ends,* names some of the places where kids have placed a bandage to protect a cut or scrape. Have children talk about accidents they have had, such as falling from their bike or being scratched by an animal, and then write about the experience.

Ask children to draw a large picture of themselves showing their full body from head to toe. Then hand each student an adhesive bandage, to be strategically placed on the picture to help tell their story.

Your brainstorming word list might include:

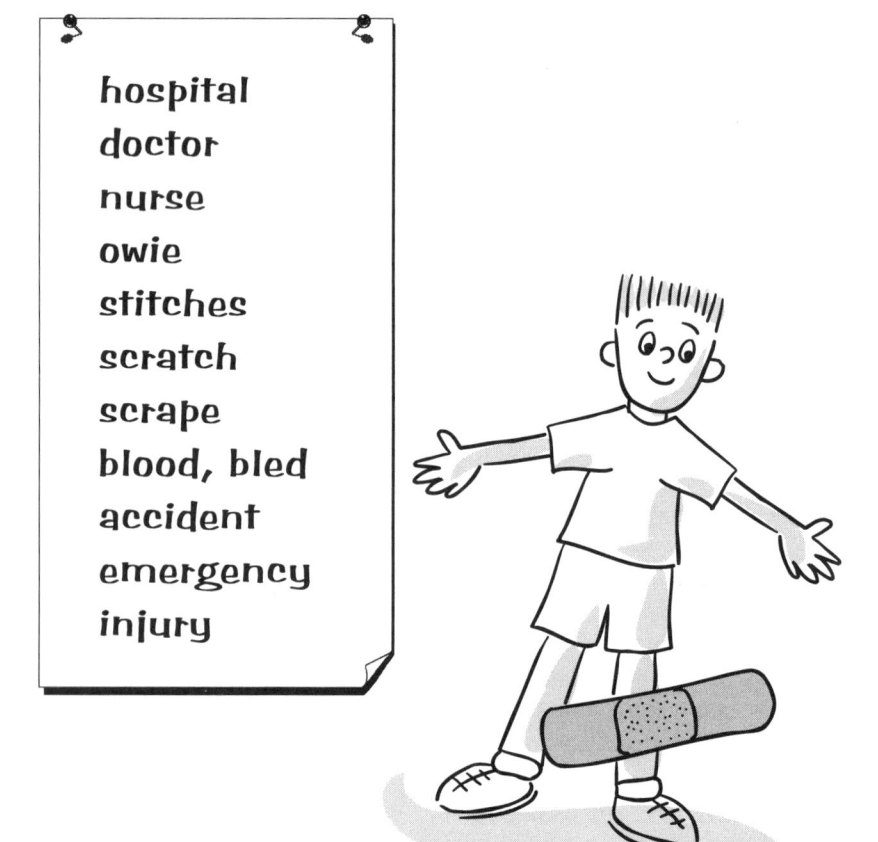

hospital
doctor
nurse
owie
stitches
scratch
scrape
blood, bled
accident
emergency
injury

Name _____ **Date** _____

Quick! I need a bandage! Here's what happened.

I'm in Big Trouble

Nina Payne has written a poem entitled "Bubble Gum." This poem can be found in *The Random House Book of Poetry for Children*. It tells all about getting in trouble because of a wad of sticky gum. The gum sticks to the bubble-blower's nose, toes, and hair. Lead a discussion of ways in which children have gotten into trouble, not necessarily with a wad of gum. Let their imaginations (and memories) run wild before they write about their own version of trouble.

Look for children's poetry collections written by Brod Bagert, such as *If Only I Could Fly*, *Let Me Be . . . the Boss*, and *Chicken Socks*. His poems are written from the child's point of view, and they allow the child to express emotions and ideas while being humorous. Many of Bagert's poems fit nicely into "All About Me" prompts.

Name _____ **Date** _____

I'm in big trouble now. It all happened when . . .

_____
_____
_____
_____
_____
_____
_____
_____
_____
_____
_____
_____
_____
_____
_____
_____
_____
_____
_____
_____
_____
_____

Jealousy

Everyone feels jealousy at one time or another. In Marc Brown's book, *Arthur's Chicken Pox,* DW is jealous of her brother because, due to his illness, he gets all of the attention from Grandma. DW ends up pretending that she also has the chicken pox to get her share of attention. The book has a funny twist in the end, when DW actually does get chicken pox!

Lead a discussion centering around the feelings of jealousy children have experienced. Jealousy may have resulted from a sibling getting attention, as in the Arthur story, or it may have resulted from a friend getting a part in a play, for example. Jealousy may be the result of being left at home with a sitter when parents took a trip. Discuss the subject and then ask students to write their own stories.

Name _____ **Date** _____

I felt jealous when . . .

Something Made Me Smile

A poem by Winifred J. Mott, "The Smile," is found in the *Poetry Place Anthology*. It is a whimsical comparison of a smile and a scowl. Located on the same page is a poem by Lee Blair called "The Big Laugh." Either one or both of these poems could be used to lead into a discussion of something that makes us smile.

Have children write about something that makes them smile. It could be something that happened today or a while ago. It could be something that a teacher or friend or family member said or did. It might be something that they saw on their way to school. Have them describe the event and tell how it made them feel.

Name _____ **Date** _____

I smiled when . . .

_____
_____
_____
_____
_____
_____
_____
_____
_____
_____
_____
_____
_____
_____
_____
_____
_____
_____
_____
_____
_____
_____
_____
_____

I Helped in the Kitchen

Many children have kitchen chores. Maybe they clear the table when a meal is finished. Or they help wash and dry the dishes. Or they even do some of the cooking! Anthony Browne's *Piggybook* tells about a family that would not help Mother with chores around the house. The house became a pigsty when Mother left home to teach them a lesson, but she returned later in the story. The family learns a valuable lesson—that everyone needs to pitch in and help with the household chores, in this delightfully illustrated story.

Have children write about a time when they helped around the house. It might be a cleaning task or it might be cooking something. Ask them how good a job they did, and were they ever asked to help out again? Were they really good helpers?

Name _____ **Date** _____

I help around the house by . . .

Making Someone Else Happy

Eileen Spinelli has written a special book entitled *Somebody Loves You, Mr. Hatch*. Mr. Hatch is a person who lives his life pretty much by himself. One day a box of Valentine candy is mistakenly given to him along with a note that says "Somebody loves you." He begins to smile and talk to people and do things for people because he thinks somebody cares about him. When he finds out that the candy really belongs to someone else, he is sad and goes back to living a lonely life. But his neighbors realize how much they all care about him and want him to be happy. This touching story makes a good point about how we can make other people happy through our actions and our words.

Discuss with children the kinds of things that make other people happy. Ask them what we can do to bring a smile to someone else's face. Brainstorm a list of ideas. Then ask them to write about something they will do to make someone smile.

Name _____ **Date** _____

Today I'm going to make someone smile by . . .

Things I Can't Part With

One person's treasure is another person's trash. We all have special things that give us pleasure. No one would dare sell them at a garage sale! Joy Watson's book, *Grandpa's Slippers,* tells about a pair of slippers that Grandpa doesn't want to give up. Have children think about something they don't want to part with and write about it. In Watson's story, it happens to be an item of clothing, but their item might be a stuffed animal or a toy or perhaps a baby blanket.

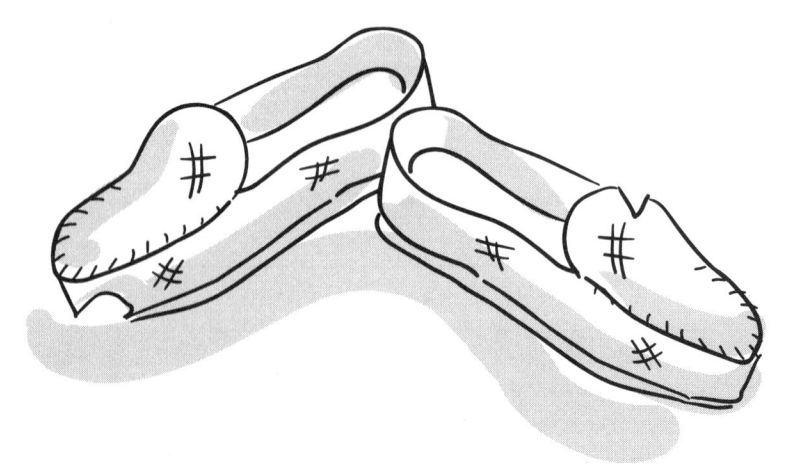

Name _____ **Date** _____

Please don't ask me to give up my . . .

Daily Writing Prompts: **All About Me**

I Lost a Tooth

Arthur's Tooth, by Marc Brown, deals with wanting to lose a first tooth. Arthur can't wait for it to happen! For many children, losing a first tooth happens in kindergarten or first grade. Most children in the elementary grades will have had the experience of losing a tooth. Some may have lost several.

Have children write a story about losing a tooth. Ask them how and when it happened. Where were they at the time? What happened to the tooth? Did they put it under their pillow? What was the result?

Brainstorming words might include:

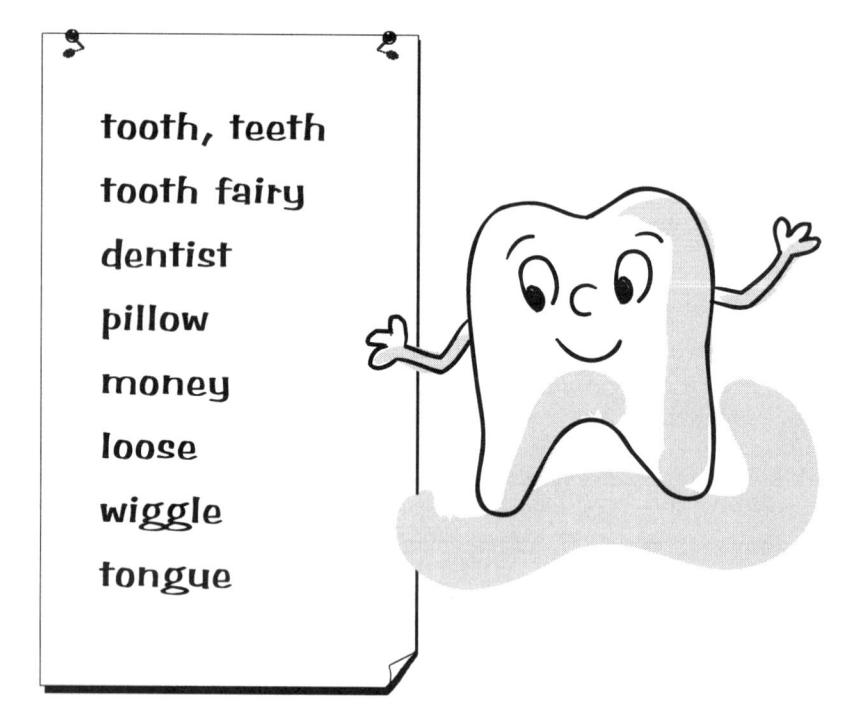

tooth, teeth
tooth fairy
dentist
pillow
money
loose
wiggle
tongue

Name _____ **Date** _____

I lost a tooth! Here's what happened . . .

A Tricky Situation

Tops & Bottoms, by Janet Stevens, tells a funny story about a rabbit who plays a trick on a bear. The rabbit promises to share the produce from the garden with the bear, but the bear always get the short end of the deal.

Ask children to think about a time they played a trick on someone. It might have been a magic trick they learned from someone. It might have been an April Fools' joke that worked. Tell them to write about their experience.

Name _____ **Date** _____

I played a trick on somebody! . . .

Sibling Rivalries

The Pain and the Great One, by Judy Blume, expresses some of the feelings that children have about their brothers and sisters. At one time or another, nearly all of us have felt that a sibling or someone else was loved more than we were. Because of jealous feelings, children have often done things that made them a "pain" to other family members.

Discuss the ideas in Blume's book or a similar story line. Ask children to write about a time that they were a "pain" to someone else because they were jealous.

Name _____ **Date** _____

Sometimes I can be a pain when . . .

_____
_____
_____
_____
_____
_____
_____
_____
_____
_____
_____
_____
_____
_____
_____
_____
_____
_____
_____
_____
_____

Daily Writing Prompts: **All About Me**

My Favorite Tree

Harry Behn's book *Trees,* which is also a familiar poem, is a simple tribute to "... the kindest things I know...." Trees provide us with so much simple pleasure. They give us shade. They cool us off on a hot day. Their branches are the perfect place to hang a swing or to build a tree house.

Have children think about a favorite tree. It might be in their yard, or it might be in a park. Ask them to write about their tree and tell why they like it. Have they climbed their tree? If so, how does it feel to climb into its branches and look down on the world below? Do they climb their tree with friends, or do they like to ascend into its branches alone? What do they like to do while they are in or near their tree? Do they read a good book? Or, do they just sit and think about things?

Name _____ **Date** _____

I like my favorite tree because . . .

Favorite Foods

There are many poems and books about food. A favorite is *Bread and Jam for Frances,* by Russell Hoban. Frances wants to eat nothing but bread and jam, three meals a day, until her mother stops asking her if she wants to eat the meal she has prepared. Frances learns a good lesson about eating a variety of different foods.

Talk about foods that children like to eat. Have them imagine eating nothing but bacon and eggs or spaghetti and meatballs for a week. Ask them what food they would want to eat every day for a week.

In the "Miscellaneous Writing Prompts" section of this book you will find directions for making reversible books. This format would be useful when writing about "Foods I Like vs. Foods I Don't Like."

Name _____ **Date** _____

I could eat nothing but _____ for a week!

Daily Writing Prompts: **All About Me**

Boy Did I Mess Up!

In Helen Lester's book *Listen Buddy,* a little rabbit gets messages all mixed up because he doesn't listen carefully. Buddy's parents ask him to bring them a variety of things, but because Buddy doesn't listen, he always brings the wrong things—like potatoes instead of tomatoes. But when Buddy messes up and brings the wrong things to the Scruffy Varmint, he realizes he needs to listen carefully.

Have children think about a time when they didn't listen carefully and something got messed up. Ask them what they were supposed to do, and what happened when they didn't follow directions. Did they learn a lesson from the experience? Have them write about it.

Name _____ **Date** _____

I messed up when I was supposed to . . .

Everybody Had to Wait for Me

Pig William, by Arlene Dubanevich, is a cute story about a pig who keeps his siblings waiting even though they are anxious to get to the park for a picnic. William takes a bath and brushes his teeth and feeds his fish and does a number of other things just because he really doesn't want to go to the park. In the end, everyone leaves for the park and William stays home. But, William has his own fun without the others.

Ask children if there was ever a time when they kept someone waiting because they really didn't want to go somewhere or do something. Maybe they didn't want to go to school. Or they didn't want to go to bed. What did they do to try to get out of it? Did the stalling work? What happened when they finally did whatever it was they wanted to avoid? Did they have a good time after all? Have children write about such an experience.

Name _____ **Date** _____

I kept someone waiting because . . .

My Homework Routine

Many students have a regular routine for completing homework assignments. In Russell Hoban's poem "Homework," found in *The Random House Book of Poetry for Children*, the author refers to homework in this way: "Homework has the smell of Monday. . . ." Some children will be able to relate to this idea. For some, homework is not thought to be a pleasant undertaking. It is sometimes dreaded, just like having to get up on Monday mornings to go to school.

Have children think about their homework routine. Ask them to write a paragraph that tells when they are expected to work on homework, and any tactics they have tried to postpone it. If they don't have a homework routine, here's an opportunity for you to discuss ways to help them get their homework done.

Name _____ **Date** _____

I try to do my homework . . .

Nobody Listens to Me

If you asked the children whether they thought adults listened to them, the response would probably be no. Children think adults do not pay attention to them when they have something important to say or tell. In the book *Nobody Listens to Andrew*, by Elizabeth Guilfoile, the boy has found a bear in his room. Nobody will listen to him when he tries to tell about it. Finally he has to shout it out.

Have children think about a time when they thought nobody was listening. What were they trying to say or tell? Did they ever get their message told? Who listened? And what happened as a result? Ask them to write about their experience.

Name _____ **Date** _____

Nobody would listen to me when . . .

Lost and Found

In Beatrix Potter's classic tale, Peter Rabbit loses his coat in Farmer MacGregor's garden. In the poem "The Three Little Kittens," the trio loses their mittens. In Jan Brett's *The Mitten*, a boy loses his mitten and a group of animals moves into it. There are many stories and poems about losing things. Luckily, the lost items are usually found and the stories end happily.

Have children imagine losing a shoe and they can't leave the house without it. Time is running out! Where would they look? Where could that shoe, or other lost item, possibly be? Ask them to write a story that tells about something they lost. What happened as a result? Where did they finally find the item?

Daily Writing Prompts: **All About Me**

Name _____ **Date** _____

Oh, dear! I've lost my . . .

I Can't Fall Asleep

Ask children if they are sometimes afraid to go to sleep at night. Are they ever afraid that there's a monster under their bed or in their closet? Do they ever think that there is a creature outside the window? In Jim Aylesworth's book *Teddy Bear Tears*, a little boy has to convince himself that everything is okay and that it is safe to go to sleep. By comforting his teddy bears, one at a time, he is finally ready to go to sleep.

Ask children what they do on a night when they cannot go to sleep. Do they count sheep? Do they talk to their teddy bears or other stuffed animals? Do they turn on a flashlight and read under the covers until they get sleepy? Have them write about trying to get to sleep at night.

Name _____ **Date** _____

When I can't get to sleep I like to . . .

My Favorite Book

Byrd Baylor's *Everybody Needs a Rock* is a wonderfully descriptive book about finding the perfect rock. Most kids have found a rock that they think is special. They want to share it at show-and-tell time. They like to tell where they got it and what makes it so special. Here is an opportunity for them to write a descriptive passage about the perfect rock. Is it round or oblong? Is it rough or smooth? Does it have rough edges? Does it remind them of something else? What color is it? Where did they find it? Have them answer these questions as they write about their rock.

Name _____ **Date** _____

My favorite rock looks like this . . .

_____
_____
_____
_____
_____
_____
_____
_____
_____
_____
_____
_____
_____
_____
_____
_____
_____
_____
_____
_____
_____
_____
_____
_____

Daily Writing Prompts: **All About Me**

I Want to Look Different

Ask children if there is something about them that they would like to change. Maybe they think their hair should be a different color. Or that their freckles look funny. Or maybe they wish they did not have to wear glasses.

Arthur is unhappy about his nose in *Arthur's Nose*, by Marc Brown. He tries on a variety of noses but can't find one that seems to look any better. Have children write about something that they would like to change about their appearance.

Name _____ **Date** _____

It would be great if I could just change . . .

Sometimes I Feel Like an Animal

Ask children if they sometimes feel "growly," like a dog, or feel sly, like a fox. *Sometimes I Feel Like a Mouse,* by Jeanne Modesitt, suggests that children might take on characteristics of animals. For example, "Sometimes I feel like an elephant stomping BOLD." Each page of the book contains an animal and a word that describes how one might feel.

Have children imagine themselves as an animal and then write about it. Help them brainstorm words that describe the way they would move, sound, look, and/or feel. Collect children's writing and make a class book about the subject.

Name _____ **Date** _____

Sometimes I feel like a . . .

Daily Writing Prompts: **All About Me**

My Favorite Place to Be Alone

In Eve Bunting's *Secret Place*, a child tells about a place in the middle of a big city. The boy sees beauty in a place that others might not think about. Ask children to describe a secret place where they like to go when they want peace and quiet. Have they shared their special place with anyone? Have children write a descriptive paragraph about their favorite place to go when they want to be alone.

Name _____ **Date** _____

I have a secret place to go whenever I . . .

When I Grow Up

Mary Pope Osborne, Laurence Yep, and others have written stories from their own childhood memories in a book entitled *When I Was Your Age: Original Stories About Growing Up.* The stories are sometimes funny and sometimes heartbreaking. They express feelings familiar to many children.

Ask children to think about the future. Where might they be and what might they be doing in twenty years? In the book *Little Nino's Pizzeria,* by Karen Barbour, the little boy thinks he will take over his father's restaurant some day. Ask them what they think they will do or hope they will do in the future.

Name _____ **Date** _____

In twenty years, I will be grown up, and I will be . . .

When I Was Little

It's interesting the way children mature when they enter school. Suddenly their prior experiences are all ". . . when I was little." Frank Asch has written stories about a young, innocent bear who does not understand the ways of the world. *Bear Shadow, Sand Cake, Milk and Cookies,* and *Moon Cake* are all good stories about this innocent, childlike bear.

Ask children what strange things they thought were true when they were little. Did they think that their stuffed animals could talk? Did they think that the moon was made of cheese? Did they think that grown-ups could do anything? Have them write about something that they once believed was true.

Name _____ **Date** _____

When I was little, I thought that . . .

I'm a Bookworm

Children who love to read are able to find out so many fun and interesting things. Those who are bookworms are indeed lucky. They discover favorite authors and favorite books. If you ask them, they will tell you just how long they have been bookworms and how they got started! Discuss how it feels to be a bookworm and then ask your children to write about it.

Notice that the prompt is designed in a circular shape. This will facilitate making a class accordion bookworm out of the stories. Mount them on individual circles made of sturdy paper cut slightly larger than the writing paper; tape the segments together and then fold the segments accordion style. Add a circular head with eyes and antennae and a tail at the end. If students have written stories that require more pieces of circular paper, they can be stapled together on a single caterpillar segment so pages can be turned. Place your accordion book on top of a bookshelf for easy viewing and reading.

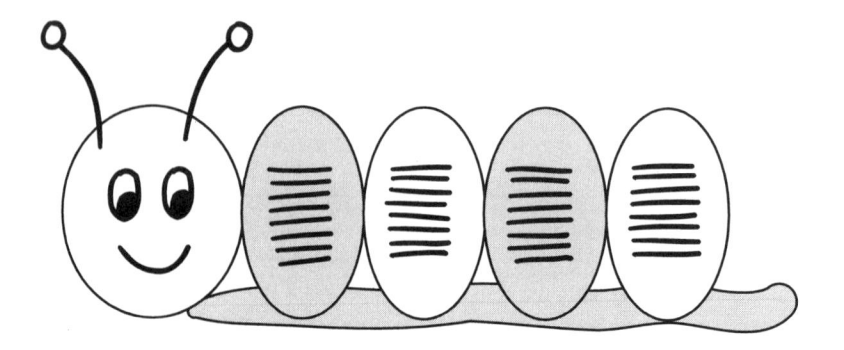

Name _____

Date _____

There is no doubt about it. I'm a bookworm!

_____

_____

_____

_____

_____

_____

_____

_____

_____

_____

_____

_____

_____

My Favorite Books

Share "Reading Books," a poem by Vivian G. Gouled, which can be found in the *Poetry Place Anthology*. This poem mentions all kinds of books that children like to read. Actually, you will find three pages dedicated to "Book Friends" in the above-mentioned anthology. The choice of a poem to lead the book discussion is up to you.

Ask children to think about the kinds of books they like to read. Do they enjoy fiction, nonfiction, history, adventure? When they go to the library or bookstore, do they look in a specific section first? Ask children to write about the kinds of books they like to read.

Name _____ **Date** _____

The books that I like best are . . .

Books Can Take You Anywhere!

If you ask children about the books they like to read, you can start a good discussion of numerous places that stories can take you. In *The Random House Book of Poetry for Children* you will find Barbara A. Huff's poem entitled "The Library." The building itself is described as one that looks like any other building you might pass on the street, but it is what's inside that makes the library a magical place.

Some children like to read books that take them back to the time of the dinosaurs. Others like to read about pirates or sea animals. Ask children to write about places they have seen in books that they would like to visit. You might want to invite students to draw a scene from a favorite book to inspire thoughts about places they would like to visit.

Name _____ **Date** _____

Books can take me anywhere! I would like to visit . . .

A Funny Thing Happened at School

With any hope, children will never fear their teacher as does the child in *The Teacher from the Black Lagoon*, by Mike Thaler. When the child in this story actually meets his teacher, he discovers a very caring and kind person.

We should all laugh at the teacher depicted in Thaler's book. We need to be able to laugh with children and show them that there is humor in life and in learning. Ask children to think about something funny that happened at school. What or who made them laugh? Could it have been their teacher? When and where did it happen? Have them write about a funny thing that happened at school.

Name _____ **Date** _____

A funny thing happened at school . . .

Show-and-Tell

There are few things in school that are awaited with as much anticipation as show-and-tell. Students love to bring in their little items to share. Some will stop along the way to school on show-and-tell day to find a rock or feather or ANYTHING just so they might have something to share.

Kevin Henkes' book, *Lilly's Purple Plastic Purse,* is a delightful story about show-and-tell. Lilly could not wait to show her new purse and the items she carried inside. She managed to get into some trouble because of her excitement and inability to wait until the proper time.

Ask children to think about something they wanted to share on show-and-tell day. What sort of item was it? Where did they get it? What was so special about the item? Have them write a story about a special show-and-tell day.

Name _____ Date _____

For show-and-tell I brought . . .

Trouble at School

In a previous prompt we asked children to write about something funny that happened at school. This prompt has a slightly different slant. Here we ask children to write about a problem at school. It might be a problem with friends or with a teacher. In the book *Arthur's Teacher Trouble*, by Marc Brown, the focus is on a problem Arthur has with his teacher. In another book in the Arthur series, *Arthur's April Fool*, there are problems with another child. Luckily, the problems are resolved in both books.

Ask children to think about something that caused a problem for them at school. Have them write about the problem and tell how it was resolved. A discussion should follow that centers on how to resolve the troublesome situations that all children experience.

Daily Writing Prompts: **All About Me**

Name _____ **Date** _____

I had a problem at school when . . .

My Friend Moved Away

If your school classroom is typical, you have children who come and go. They stay long enough to form friendships but then some must move to another school for one reason or another. The Judith Viorst poem "Since Hanna Moved Away," from *The Random House Book of Poetry for Children*, expresses sadness at losing a good friend. The feelings of loss expressed have been felt by many. Viorst says that since a good friend moved away ". . . Chocolate ice cream tastes like prunes. . . ." and ". . . The sky is grouch gray. . . ."

Discuss the feelings children have had when they lost (or would have if they lost) a good friend. Have them write a story, real or imagined, about a friend who moved away. Have them consider the following: Is there a happy ending to the story? Do the friends stay in touch through sending letters or even visiting one another? Does the writer make a new friend to help heal the loss of the absent one?

Name _____ **Date** _____

When a good friend moves away I feel . . .

I'm Not Going to Move!

The previous prompt concerned a friend who moved away. Turn that thought around and have children consider their own family making a move. Here is a chance for them to practice their best persuasive writing in an effort to convince their family how important it is to stay put.

Alexander, Who's Not (Do you hear me? I mean it!) Going to Move, by Judith Viorst, tells the story of a boy who has to finally give in to the idea of moving away. But he fights it valiantly, at least in his thoughts!

This will probably be a fictitious situation for your children, unless one is facing a move in the near future. Have them pretend that their family must move away. Ask them to write a story that tells where they will go as well as why. Encourage them to persuade their family that the move is not really necessary. Have them tell how they will get their family to stay put.

Name _____ **Date** _____

I don't want to move away because . . .

Little Kids Can Do a Lot

In Edward Marshall's book, *Four on the Shore,* four young children try to tell scary stories at their camp-out. The three older children tell their stories, which are not very scary, first. Then, the youngest child tells a story that really scares the older ones. The story is a big surprise to the older kids because they assume that a little kid cannot scare them. "Little kids are full of surprises!"

Ask children to think about a time that a little kid did something that really took them by surprise. Have them write a story about the event.

Name _____ **Date** _____

A little kid really surprised me when . . .

Taking Care of a Younger Child

Children who have younger siblings will often tell about having to watch that little brother or sister for one reason or another. It might have been for only a few minutes or it might have been for a longer period of time. In James Marshall's *Fox on the Job,* Fox's little sister causes problems when she does the unexpected. She always seems to give Fox a hard time. Fox, like a good brother would, takes it all in stride even though he wishes he did not have to bring his sister along when he goes out to play.

Even children who do not have younger siblings might have younger cousins or neighborhood children that they have had to watch. Discuss taking care of, and watching out for, little ones. Then ask children to write about a time when they had to take care of, or watch out for, a younger child. What happened? Was the situation funny? Did they really have a good time after all?

Name _____ **Date** _____

I had to look after my _____ and . . .

I Was Embarrassed

Younger siblings (or little cousins or neighborhood children) can do things that are embarrassing. It might be because they are messy when they eat. It might be because they don't talk correctly yet or that they use funny, made-up words. In the book *Little Brother's Haircut,* by Joy Cowley, an embarrassing situation takes place at the barbershop. The little brother causes quite a disturbance and ends up with only half of a haircut!

Have children think about an embarrassing situation that a younger child caused. What happened? Where did it happen? Was it funny? Was it scary? Ask them to write a story that tells about this embarrassing situation.

Name _____ **Date** _____

I was so embarrassed when . . .

A Visit with the Relatives

Summer time is great for visiting relatives. Sometimes it means a trip to another location. Sometimes the relatives come to our own house to spend a few days or more. In *The Relatives Came,* by Cynthia Rylant, the author uses descriptive passages to help us understand how sounds and smells change when other people are in a house. Ask children to close their eyes as you read some of the descriptive passages. Have them imagine the kinds of sounds and smells the author describes. Most children will have had similar experiences.

Ask children to write about a time they visited relatives, whether at their relatives' home or in their own home. Encourage them to be descriptive about the new sounds and smells experienced as a result of the visit.

Daily Writing Prompts: **All About Me**

Name _____ **Date** _____

I love it when we get to see my relatives . . .

The Old Days

In *The Day Gogo Went to Vote,* written by Elinor Batezat Sisulu and beautifully illustrated by Sharon Wilson, Gogo (Grandma) recalls the old days in Africa. She tells her grandchildren about her experiences. One day the opportunity to vote presents itself for the first time. Through this story, we are reminded of the priceless knowledge and experiences that our elders have to share. They are our windows to the past. We should let them share their experiences so that they live on.

Ask children to think about something that their grandparents or older neighbors have told them about "the olden days." Have them write about the ways life was different then.

Name _____ **Date** _____

My _____ told me this about the old days . . .

Daily Writing Prompts: **All About Me**

When I'm Big

The child in the story *When I'm Big,* by Debi Gliori, doesn't want to go to bed. He thinks about the things he will do when he is big and doesn't have to go to bed early. This is a great pattern book to parody by making writing prompts out of the sentences. For example, model the sentence in the book: ". . . When I'm big, I'm going to ride a real bike instead of a tricycle. . . ." Ask children to complete the "When I'm big. . . ." prompt on the next page. Note the addition of drawing space so they can illustrate their thoughts.

Discuss the idea of "being big." Brainstorm a list of things the children want to do when they are big. This is a good exercise to collect for a class book. Or, you might also ask each child to come up with five ideas of his or her own, illustrate them, and then make individual books.

Name _____ Date _____

When I'm big . . .

_____
_____
_____
_____
_____
_____
_____
_____
_____
_____

I'm a Unique Individual

Tacky the Penguin, by Helen Lester, is a story about a penguin who is very different from his companions. He looks different and he reacts differently to the same situations that his companions encounter.

Discuss with children what makes someone an individual. Everyone has unique characteristics and qualities. Ask them to think about themselves. Ask what characteristics and/or qualities they have that make them an individual. Have them draw a picture of themselves and then write about their uniqueness—what makes them special. The responses to this prompt make a nice class book.

Name _____ **Date** _____

I'm a unique person because . . .

_____
_____
_____
_____
_____
_____
_____
_____
_____

I'm a Late Bloomer

In *Leo the Late Bloomer,* by Robert Kraus, poor Leo has difficulty learning to read, write, and draw. Even the way he eats his food shows that he is immature. Finally Leo "blooms" and can do things like the big kids can do.

Children mature at different ages and different speeds. Some are still quite immature in first grade. The story of Leo should help children realize that they will mature, and they will be able to do things that their peers can do.

Talk about tasks that your children can do now that they could not do last year. Each grade level presents new challenges to children. Talk about those challenges and how the students have managed to learn many new things. Then ask them to write about some of the new discoveries they have made recently.

Name _____ **Date** _____

I'm learning to do new things every day!

I Can Teach You Something

As unique individuals, we all have our strengths and talents. If given the opportunity, we could all teach someone else how to do something. Maybe it would be teaching someone how to catch a baseball. Perhaps it would be teaching someone how to ride a bike. Maybe a friend can teach you how to draw a lion or a horse. In Tony Johnston's book *Amber on the Mountain,* a child named Anna teaches her friend Amber how to read.

Discussion and brainstorming should center around children's individual talents. Talk about the things that they know how to do well. What could they teach someone else how to do? Have them write about their special talent and include some of their tips for teaching someone how to do something.

Name _____ **Date** _____

I'm really good at . . .

_____
_____
_____
_____
_____
_____
_____
_____
_____
_____
_____
_____
_____
_____
_____
_____
_____
_____
_____
_____

Sometimes I Don't Feel Very Smart

Patricia Polacco is a very talented writer. Her stories often bring to life events that happened in her own childhood. You undoubtedly will enjoy sharing the heartwarming story of her struggle to learn how to read. *Thank You, Mr. Falker* is the true story of how Patricia finally learned to read in the fifth grade. Because of her reading problem, she was teased and called "dummy" and "toad" by her classmates during her elementary school years. This book is dedicated as a thank-you to the teacher who made such a dramatic change in her life.

Every child has felt inadequate at one time or another. New skills can be a real challenge until they are mastered. Discuss with children times they felt inferior because they couldn't read well, couldn't add and subtract well, or struggled to learn the alphabet or dribble a basketball or ride a bike. Talk about the kinds of things that children had trouble learning and then ask them to respond to the following prompt.

Name _____ **Date** _____

I had trouble learning . . .

A Childhood Friend

Many children have stuffed animals at home that were their best friends during early childhood. Kevin Henkes has written a book entitled *Owen*, about a little boy who has a stuffed animal named Fuzzy. Owen's mom and dad are concerned because Fuzzy goes everywhere with Owen. They wonder what will happen when Owen is old enough to go to school. In the end, Mom has a very clever solution to the problem.

Talk about favorite stuffed animals or blankets that the children used to carry around with them. How did it feel to have to leave their "friend" behind when it was time to start school? Did some children have invisible friends that they played with when they were little? Were these invisible friends humanlike or did they have imaginative animal characteristics? Talk about childhood "friends" and then have them respond to the writing prompt.

Name _____ **Date** _____

When I was little, my best friend was a . . .

Daily Writing Prompts: **All About Me**

Guess What Is in the Bag

Imagine being blind. Imagine a world that is full of darkness. You would have to compensate for your lack of sight by strengthening your senses of smell, touch, taste, and hearing. People who are blind have a unique awareness of their surroundings. *Through Grandpa's Eyes,* by Patricia MacLachlan, is the story of a child whose grandfather cannot see. Grandfather helps the child understand the smells and sounds that are so important to a person who is visually impaired.

Put an unidentified object in a drawstring bag. The object should be something that has a distinct feel, smell, and/or sound. Close the drawstring. Let children reach into the bag and feel the contents. They may shake the bag to see if the item produces a sound. They may smell the bag to see if there is a distinct aroma. Have children write what they think the item in the bag is.

Name _____ **Date** _____

I think there is a _____ in the bag because . . .

_____
_____
_____
_____
_____
_____
_____
_____
_____
_____
_____
_____
_____
_____
_____
_____
_____
_____
_____
_____
_____
_____
_____

An Overnight Visit

Ira Sleeps Over, by Bernard Waber, is a favorite story about getting ready for a sleepover at a friend's house. Ira cannot decide whether to take his teddy bear to Reggie's house. Ira's sister keeps telling him that Reggie will make fun of him if he brings a stuffed animal for bedtime.

Share the story of Ira and then initiate a discussion about any sleepovers the children have experienced, whether with a friend or relative. Talk about games they played and other things they did to have fun before it was time to turn out the lights. Did they take a teddy bear or other stuffed animal with them for the sleepover? Have the students write a story about their experiences or make up a story about an imagined sleepover.

Daily Writing Prompts: **All About Me**

Name _____ **Date** _____

I had fun when I stayed overnight with . . .

House Rules

Classrooms have rules of conduct. Many teachers like to list them on chart paper and refer to them when a student breaks a rule. Likewise, parents have house rules. The mother in Audrey Wood's book *Heckedy Peg* has told her seven children some very important rules to follow when she must leave the house to go to the market. Of course the children break the rules and find themselves in a lot of trouble. The problem is resolved in the end, but not before Mother must do some quick thinking to save her children.

Talk about school rules and relate them to rules that children should follow in their own homes. Most will be able to list a variety of rules they must follow at home. Some will have difficulty coming up with any restrictions that are put on their behavior at home! Brainstorm a list of rules that seem to be good representative "house rules" and the consequences of breaking them. Ask children to write about rules at their house and an experience they had when a rule was broken.

Daily Writing Prompts: **All About Me**

Name _____ **Date** _____

When I'm at home I know that I shouldn't . . .

146 Daily Writing Prompts: **Celebrations and Seasons**

Celebrations and Seasons

The writing prompts in this section tend to follow themes of seasonal happenings and times of celebration. Writing prompts that deal with times of celebration are for Thanksgiving and Mother's Day. These are celebrations that nearly all children observe in a similar fashion. It is hoped that the prompts that are included for these special days are written in a way that will appeal to the vast majority of children. Note that the celebration prompts themselves do not refer specifically to the particular celebration. Instead, they are generic and can be used at another time, if desired.

Thanksgiving—Turkey Tricks

Present the following poem to help children get ideas for writing a story about a turkey that escapes the carving knife.

Fat Turkey

Gobble, gobble, turkey,
You'd better run away.
The farmer's wife is planning
To cook you on Thanksgiving Day.
If you're a smart fat turkey
You'll get away . . . and quick!
Or the farmer's hungry children
Will fight over your drumstick!

Have children discuss how the turkey can get away or hide somewhere until Thanksgiving Day is over. Suggest that the turkey might trick the farmer by hiding behind a tree, or it might run away to the zoo. Let children's imaginations run wild and the ideas will come out! Have them write a paragraph about the turkey's quest by using the following prompt.

Daily Writing Prompts: **Celebrations and Seasons**

Name _____ **Date** _____

Look out, turkey! Here comes the farmer!

Mother's Day—Letters of Appreciation

The poem "On Mother's Day," by Eileen Fisher, from *The Random House Book of Poetry for Children*, gives a lovely tribute to this holiday. Readers will be inspired to take the time to make cards and presents for their mothers/grandmothers/caregivers.

Ask children what makes a mother special. What does she do for you? What can you do to make her day a little bit easier than most days? Have them write their mother, grandmother, or caregiver a letter and tell her how special she is. Encourage children to tell her what they can do to make this Mother's Day special for her.

The letter format on the following page can also be used when writing a birthday note to someone or as a note to a friend, telling him or her why they are so special.

Dear _____,

You are special because . . .

_____
_____
_____
_____
_____
_____
_____
_____
_____
_____
_____
_____
_____
_____
_____
_____

Love,

_____

My Favorite Weather

There are many different kinds of weather. We see sun, rain, snow, cloudy days, and windy days. Some days are gray and some are bright and cheerful. Talk about different kinds of weather. Most children probably prefer a sunny, warm day, but some children like rainy days. Some prefer snow so they can go sledding or skiing. Have children write about their favorite type of weather.

Thunder Cake, by Patricia Polacco, and *Listen to the Rain*, by Bill Martin, Jr., are two examples of weather books. Poems you could share might include "Fog," by Carl Sandburg, and "April Rain Song," by Langston Hughes. Both can be found in *The Random House Book of Poetry for Children*.

Name _____ **Date** _____

It's my kind of day when the weather . . .

Time for School to Begin

Parents and children alike look forward to the beginning of a new school year. Anticipation begins as soon as the stores display colorful bookbags and school supplies. Children are eager to get back to their old friends. Parents look forward to a normal routine once again.

The poem "School," by Winifred C. Marshall, in *Poetry Place Anthology*, deals with saying "Good-bye to summer," and "Hello" to a new school year. Brainstorm with children a list of things that alert them that school is about to begin. Seeing new school supplies in the stores provides a clue. So does shopping for new clothes and shoes. What else happens that signals the end of summer and the beginning of a school year? Ask children to write about getting ready for school.

Following the getting ready for school prompt, you will find prompts for each of the seasons with the same format: "You know it's time for . . . ." Discuss the signs of each season to inspire writing ideas. Look for appropriate poems or trade books to help also.

Name _____ **Date** _____

You know it's time for school to begin when . . .

Name _____ **Date** _____

You know it's time for fall to begin when . . .

Name _____ **Date** _____

You know it's time for winter to begin when . . .

Name _____ **Date** _____

You know it's time for spring to begin when . . .

Name _____ **Date** _____

You know it's time for summer to begin when . . .

Jumping in Leaves

Autumn offers a special opportunity for kids to do something that adults would probably like to do, when and if no one was looking! Children enjoy helping grown-ups rake a big pile of leaves and then taking a flying leap into the pile. It really is great fun!

Share Lois Ehlert's book *Red Leaf, Yellow Leaf*. Ehlert's colorful illustrations really bring autumn leaves to life. Try making leaves out of many colors of tissue paper. Crinkle them up and scatter them on the floor. Let children walk through them. Although this is not the same as jumping into an actual pile, it might be just the inspiration children need to write stories about jumping into leaves.

Ask children what they might find in a pile of leaves. Have them think of three or four typical things, such as nuts, feathers, or pennies, and write about them. Tell them to finish their story by finding an unusual object in the leaves. Encourage them to surprise their readers! Reproduce the prompt to allow several pages for each child. Have children illustrate each page in the space provided. Staple pages together to make individual books.

Name _____ **Date** _____

I jumped in the leaves and found . . .

_____
_____
_____
_____

Fun in the Snow

The first heavy snowfall offers a glorious treat to kids of all ages. That white fluffy blanket on the ground, with not a single mark or footprint in it, is such an inviting playground. Ezra Jack Keats' book *The Snowy Day* provides a delightful story of a child who goes outside to play in the newly fallen snow. He does a lot of things that one can do only in the snow.

Have children imagine that it snowed during the night and that there is a heavy blanket of fresh snow on the ground. Ask them what they will do when Mom finally says they can go outside and play. Have children write about their fun in the snow.

Name _____ **Date** _____

It snowed! Now I can go outside and . . .

Building Snow Creatures

Lois Ehlert's book *Snowballs* is bound to inspire ideas for all sorts of snow creatures that might be built on a snowy day. Have children make their own snow creatures out of construction paper and miscellaneous items such as buttons, ribbon, seeds, and other materials. When the snow creature has been created, ask children to write a story about their creation. Does it have a name? Will it melt or will it last all winter? Does it guard the house? Do the birds and squirrels sit on it and eat the seeds?

The second reproducible page can be used to turn the writing prompt into an expository assignment. Ask children to write about the steps necessary in creating a snow creature. They will need to tell what they made and what materials they used to make it.

Writing Prompts: **Celebrations and Seasons**

Name _____ **Date** _____

I went outside on a snowy day and I made . . .

Name _____ Date _____

Follow these steps to build a _____

First,
_____
_____

Next,
_____
_____

Finally,
_____
_____

Materials Needed:
_____
_____
_____
_____
_____
_____
_____
_____
_____
_____

Daily Writing Prompts: **Celebrations and Seasons**

Planning for Winter

In the Leo Lionni story *Frederick,* a family of mice must gather supplies to last them through the long winter. The mice gather mostly food. All are quite busy, except Frederick, who seems to just sit quietly, doing nothing. Near the end of the long winter, Frederick shares what he had been gathering. Even though it was not food to eat, Frederick provided food for thought and helped his family make it through the long, cold winter days.

Have children imagine that they have to store things for the coming winter. They will not be able to run to the store to pick up something when they need it. Ask them what they would want to have with them during the long winter months. Of course, they would need plenty of food, but what other supplies would they want and need? Have them write a list of their supplies and then support that list with a paragraph telling why they need the items.

Name _____   Date _____

I need these items during the long winter months.

_____   _____
_____   _____
_____   _____

This is why I need them.

Trouble in Winter

In Kaye Starbird's poem "Wendy in Winter," (*The Random House Book of Poetry for Children*), poor Wendy has many problems trying to get to school on a cold, slippery day. Share the poem and then ask children if they feel sorry for Wendy. Most will probably say no because Wendy brought about her own problems! Her coat blew off because it was unzipped. Her feet were cold because her boots were left at home.

Encourage students to talk about experiences they have had trying to get to school on time on a nasty-weather day. They will probably exaggerate their stories just a bit, but it is all in fun anyway. After a discussion, ask children to write a story about problems getting to school.

Although the suggested poem for this prompt deals with winter, the writing page is more generic. It might also be used the day after a storm, for example, when branches have been strewn about the streets and sidewalks.

Name _____ **Date** _____

I had trouble getting to school because . . .

Tracks in the Snow

Ask children if they have ever looked for identifiable tracks in the newly fallen snow. Did they find tracks made by birds, rabbits, and raccoons? How about dogs or human tracks? The poem "Who?," by Lilian Moore (*Poetry Place Anthology*), is a good one to share on the subject of tracks in the snow.

Have children write a story, either real or imagined, about following some tracks in the snow. Ask them where the tracks led them. Who (or what) made the tracks? Was the adventure funny or scary? Did they take someone with them—just in case they got lost or found something scary?

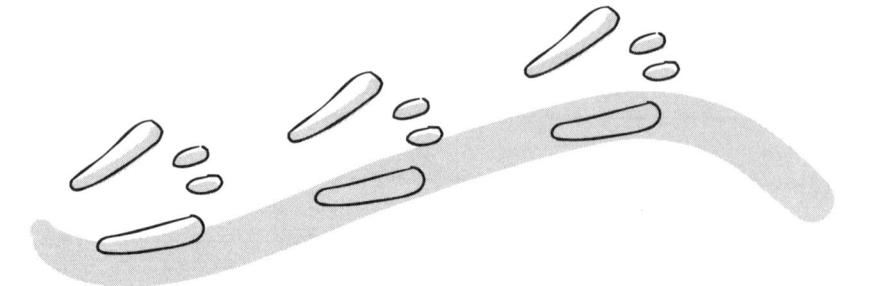

Name _____ **Date** _____

I followed some tracks in the snow and found . . .

Snowman Adventure

The snowman in Winifred C. Marshall's poem "Peter, the Snowman" (*Poetry Place Anthology*) is adorned with clothing that belongs to various members of the family. Peter, the snowman, has Daddy's hat and Cousin Sue's mittens. A snowman often wears items that give it a more human look.

Have children imagine that one of the items they placed on their snowman was magic. It brought the snowman to life! Ask them what magic item brought their snowman to life. Then have them write about the adventure they had with their snowman. Ask them where they went and what they did together. Will their snowman melt in the end, or not? Will the snowman come back next winter?

Name _____ **Date** _____

I placed a magic _____ on my snowman and it came to life!

Waiting for Spring

In cold climates, sometimes the winter months can drag on endlessly. Children get restless waiting for nice weather to return. There are so many things that cannot be done during a cold winter! "Waiting," a poem by Harry Behn (*Poetry Place Anthology*), reminds us of other living things, such as bears, bees, and seeds that wait for spring too.

Ask children if there are any kinds of activities they are waiting to do until spring finally arrives. Are they waiting to play baseball? Are they waiting to play on the swings and merry-go-round again? Are they waiting for hotter weather? Are they waiting to plant flowers or vegetables with their parents? Have them write about what they are looking forward to doing in the spring.

Name _____ **Date** _____

I can't wait for spring so that I can . . .

_____
_____
_____
_____
_____
_____
_____
_____
_____
_____
_____
_____
_____
_____
_____
_____
_____
_____
_____
_____
_____
_____

Daily Writing Prompts: **Celebrations and Seasons**

In Like a Lion, Out Like a Lamb

March weather is oftentimes a reminder of the saying "In like a lion, out like a lamb." You might be surprised at the answers you get from children if you ask them what that saying means.

For this prompt it is suggested that you *not* activate prior knowledge or do any brainstorming or discussing of the topic. This one is best when presented without any introduction. If you really want to find out what the children are thinking, just give them the prompt and read it together. That's all! Then let them write their thoughts!

Name _____ Date _____

In like a lion, out like a lamb.

I think this saying means . . .

March Winds Are Blowing

Pat Hutchins' picture book *The Wind Blew* depicts the wind blowing things around, picking up hats and umbrellas and a host of other items, and scattering them across fields and towns.

Ask children to write about a time when the wind took something away from them. What did the wind take? Where were they when it happened? Did they follow the item down the street or across the field? Where did it take them? Did they get it back? Did they find something else along the way?

Name _____ Date _____

The wind took my . . .

Rainy Day Fun

After a spring rain, there are often puddles on the sidewalks. It is fun to jump in a puddle and splash about, and it is fun to ride a bike through puddles and leave tracks on the sidewalk. Puddles are inviting places for kids and grown-ups alike.

Charlotte Pomerantz's book *The Piggy in the Puddle* will delight any child or grown-up who likes puddles. The whole pig family plays in a big puddle in an effort to get the little sister to come out of it! There are also poems that facilitate a discussion about puddles, such as "Mud," by Polly Chase Boyden, and "The Muddy Puddle," by Dennis Lee, which are both found in *The Random House Book of Poetry for Children*.

Ask children to write about a time, real or imagined, when they had fun in a puddle. Did they splash around? Did they ride their bike through it? Did they get all wet? What was their parents' reaction when they got home and were wet, perhaps even soaked to the skin?

Name _____ **Date** _____

I love to play in the puddles after a rain!

The School Year Is Ending

It is so hard to try to stay focused on papers and books when the last days of school have finally arrived. Children want to talk about their summer activities. Whether it be a trip to the beach or playing baseball, visiting the relatives or a local theme park, children want to talk about it. Why not turn talk into a writing activity!

"School," a poem by Iva Riebel Judy (*Poetry Place Anthology*), tells of a child who is excited about the end of the school year and the beginning of summer vacation. Ask children what they plan to do this summer. What makes a summer day special? Have them write about what they will do or would like to do this summer.

Name _____ **Date** _____

Now that summer is here I can . . .

Daily Writing Prompts: All Kinds of Animals

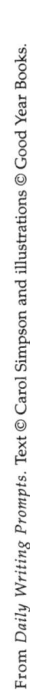

All Kinds of Animals

The section that follows contains writing prompts that are tied to animal stories and poems. You will find prompts for both fiction and nonfiction writing. You will find animals of the present and the past. You will find animals that are real and some that are not real. Some prompts ask us to imagine that animals have human abilities.

Some of the animal prompts could be used as assessment tools. After studying animal camouflage, for example, children can show their understanding of the concept by writing about themselves as an animal with natural camouflage to help it hide from its enemies. After studying the sea, children could show their understanding of underwater life by writing about themselves as a sea animal. What do they eat? How do they keep safe from their enemies?

Dinosaurs Can Help Us

Children love to read about dinosaurs. Pictures of dinosaurs are a great curiosity to many young children. They like to draw pictures of them and hear stories about them. Extend that curiosity to writing about them.

Bernard Most's *If the Dinosaurs Came Back* is filled with ideas about the ways these giant creatures might help us if they were still alive today. Share the book and then ask children to write about what they think they might do if they had a dinosaur to help them today.

Name _____ **Date** _____

A dinosaur could help me . . .

Life in the Sea

Fish Faces, by Norbert Wu, contains photographs of all kinds of sea animals. Some are pretty and colorful, and some are really quite scary looking. If you cannot locate this book, find pictures of various kinds of fish and other sea creatures that children can examine. There are several excellent nature magazines that contain spectacular photographs. There also are numerous trade books filled with facts and information about sea animals. Provide as many sources as you can so that children acquaint themselves with the subject matter.

Have children select a sea creature that they would like to be. Then have them write about themselves as that animal. What kind of creature would they be? Have them describe themselves and tell about life in the sea. How would they survive and keep safe from their enemies? What would they eat? Would they live alone or with other sea animals?

Name _____ Date _____

I live in the sea. I am . . .

Animals in Hiding

Animals can protect themselves from their enemies by various methods. One is through their body coloration. Camouflage helps a polar bear keep from being seen since its natural habitat is covered with snow and ice. Camouflage helps the chameleon hide on a leaf or on the trunk of a tree.

There are many good books on camouflage. One fictional account is Craig Kee Strete's *They Thought They Saw Him*, a story about a chameleon who hides from its enemies. Ruth Heller has written a collection of camouflage books about different types of animals. Among the titles you will find are *How to Hide a Crocodile and Other Reptiles* and *How to Hide a Polar Bear and Other Mammals*. There are also books on insects and amphibians with similar titles. *Searchin' Safari*, by Jeff O'Hare, has pictures of animals as they hide in their natural habitats. Children get to search for the hidden animals as well as read information about them within the pages of this book.

Have children select an animal that has natural camouflage and then write a story about themselves as that animal. Tell them to be sure the story shows that they understand how their animal uses its camouflage to hide from enemies.

Name _____ **Date** _____

I am a _____ and I can hide . . .

Daily Writing Prompts: **All Kinds of Animals**

Zoo Animals

In *Edward the Emu,* by Sheena Knowles, the main character does not want to be an emu because the people who visit the zoo prefer to see the seals or snakes or some other animal instead of him. This book contains whimsical illustrations by Rod Clement that show Edward trying to roar like a lion, balance a ball on his nose like a seal, and display other attention-getting behaviors.

Discuss visiting a zoo. If possible, make a visit to a local zoo. Inspire writing about a zoo visit by asking children questions. What animal do they always want to visit first? What is their favorite zoo animal? Why did they choose that one? What is so special about that animal? If there are children who have not been to a zoo, ask which animal they would want to see first. Have them use their answers to spark the following writing exercise.

Name _____ **Date** _____

My favorite zoo animal is _____ because . . .

_____
_____
_____
_____
_____
_____
_____
_____
_____
_____
_____
_____
_____
_____
_____
_____
_____
_____
_____
_____
_____
_____
_____

Animals Can Do Neat Things

Animals can do things that humans cannot do, such as live in water or fly or change their natural coloring. *The Chick and the Duckling,* by Mirra Ginsburg, is about a chick that tries to do everything a duckling can do, until it nearly drowns!

Ask children what they would like to be able to do that they cannot do now. What animal would they want to be so that they could do that? Have them write about themselves as that animal and tell what they can do now that is special. How does this special something help them in their daily life?

Name _____ **Date** _____

I wish I could be _____ so that I could . . .

Pet Problems

Many families have pets. The more typical pets include dogs and cats. Fish and birds are also popular. Some families do not have pets in spite of the pleadings of their youngsters. Of course, some can't have pets because of allergies or restrictions made by landlords.

Judith Viorst's poem "Mother Doesn't Want a Dog," (*The Random House Book of Poetry for Children*), is a good example of writing on this subject. *The Case of the Elevator Duck,* a short chapter book by Polly Berends, tells the story of a boy in an apartment complex where pets are not allowed. He finds a duck on the elevator and tries to keep it safe until he can find its owner.

Have children write a story about getting a new pet. Ask them what pet they would like to have. How would they take care of it? How would they provide food and a place for it to sleep? Remind them that they must prove themselves worthy of getting a pet, so they must be persuasive!

Name _____ **Date** _____

Please, oh please, let me get a pet _____

Lost Dog

You will find many poems about dogs in both of the recommended poetry anthologies. Select one or more poems that give good descriptions of dogs. Pay attention to the language used. Important features of dog descriptions might include their floppy ears or their constant scratching. Color, size, and breed of a dog are also important to note.

Have children imagine that they have lost their dog, either real or pretend. Ask them to write a description of their lost dog in the form of a notice to post in their neighborhood. Make sure they know that the description must be thorough enough so that someone could pick their dog out of a group.

Name _____ **Date** _____

Help! I've lost my dog! You'll know it's mine when you see it because . . .

I Need a Home

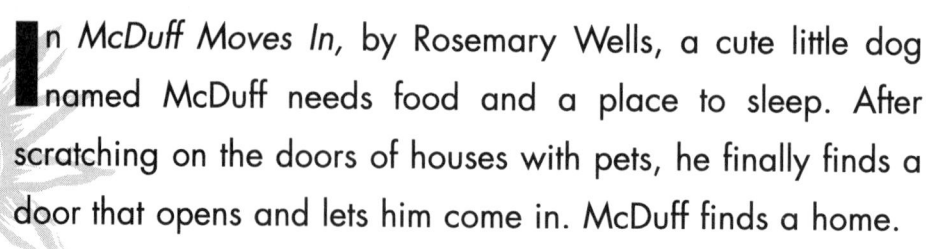

In *McDuff Moves In,* by Rosemary Wells, a cute little dog named McDuff needs food and a place to sleep. After scratching on the doors of houses with pets, he finally finds a door that opens and lets him come in. McDuff finds a home.

Have children imagine they are McDuff. Tell them they need a home. Ask them how they will get someone to open a door and let them in. Have them write about their adventure of finding a home.

Name _____ **Date** _____

If I'm going to find a home, I'll have to . . .

If Dogs Could Talk

Here is a prompt to inspire an unusual pet story. In preparation for this prompt, you may want to read aloud *Martha Speaks,* by Susan Meddaugh. This book will introduce students to the idea that their dog (or neighbor's dog) might be able to talk if given the chance!

Ask children what dogs would say if they could talk. Would the dogs only speak to their owners? Do they think animals talk to each other? Do they think talking animals tell stories about people? Have children write a story about a talking dog or another talking animal.

Name _____ **Date** _____

You probably won't believe this but my _____ talks!

_____
_____
_____
_____
_____
_____
_____
_____
_____
_____
_____
_____
_____
_____
_____
_____
_____
_____
_____
_____
_____
_____
_____
_____
_____

My Pet Mouse

Rose Fyleman, author of the poem "Mice" (*The Random House Book of Poetry for Children*), seems to like mice. Although she realizes that many people do not like mice, she still says, ". . . I think mice are nice."

Have children imagine having a mouse for a pet. Many people would not like to hold or pet their mouse. Ask them how they would convince people that their mouse is really a cute cuddly pet. What are some things they can do with their pet mouse? Would they ever use their mouse to scare someone? What is so good about having a mouse for a pet? Have children write about why having a pet mouse is the best.

Name _____ **Date** _____

My pet mouse is the best . . .

Washing My Pet

The title character of *Mrs. Wishy-Washy*, by Joy Cowley, loves to keep her farm animals clean. When she gets out her tub and brush, the animals run and hide to escape the inevitable bath.

Discuss with children the process of giving a dog (or other animal) a bath. Ask them what problems they think they might encounter. Does it matter whether the animal is big or little? Ask those who have a dog to tell what their pet does to keep from getting a bath. Some animals love to roll in the dirt right after a bath. Ask them if their pets have done this. Have them write a story about their pet or a pretend pet getting a bath.

Daily Writing Prompts: **All Kinds of Animals**

Name _____ **Date** _____

When my _____ gets a bath . . .

My Favorite Stuffed Animal

If you ask children to bring in their favorite stuffed animals, you will get a menagerie of furry creatures. You will see teddy bears, rabbits, pigs, and all kinds of animals. Share the following poem with children to promote writing about stuffed animals. Then have them write their own story about their favorite stuffed animal.

My Teddy

I love my fuzzy teddy.
He goes to bed with me.
And when I'm scared or lonely
He keeps me company.
I never have to feed him.
His needs are very few.
He only wants a friendly hug
To keep him good as new.
I'll bet you have a teddy
To snuggle up with you.
If you show me your teddy
I'll show my teddy too.

Name _____ **Date** _____

My favorite stuffed animal is . . .

Town and Country Animals

Jan Brett is but one author who has rewritten the famous tale of *The City Mouse and the Country Mouse*. Select several examples of this story and talk about their similarities and differences. A blank Venn diagram is provided for writing in the information that results from the discussion. Space is also provided for the writing of a narrative on those similarities and differences. You may fill in the Venn diagram together, with children copying the information from an example done on the board or overhead projector. The blank lines could be used as an individual assignment, one that requires writing a narrative about the stories being compared.

A prompt page is not provided for a parody of the story. However, encourage children to write their own versions on a separate sheet of paper in the form of:

> The Town Dog and the Country Dog
> The Town Cat and the Country Cat
> The Zoo Lion and the Jungle Lion
> The Pet Snake and the Forest Snake

In preparation for writing their parody, have children fill in the Venn diagram with their story ideas first.

Name _____ **Date** _____

Title _____

Story #1   Story #2

_____
_____
_____
_____
_____
_____
_____
_____
_____

Monkey Business

Curious George, the little monkey created by H. A. Rey, gets into all sorts of trouble. The man with the yellow hat pulls him out of one problem situation after another. In the end, the monkey is forgiven because he ends up doing something brave and helps, rather than harms, the people around him.

Have children imagine that they are the man with the yellow hat. They must leave the house for the morning and then George will be on his own. What should they tell George before they leave? What does George do that causes troubles? Have children write their own adventure about the curious little monkey.

Name _____ **Date** _____

The little monkey was told to be good, but . . .

Daily Writing Prompts: **All Kinds of Animals**

Daily Writing Prompts: **Fantasy**

Fantasy

This section of writing prompts relates to flights of fantasy. Ask children to imagine that they have something or are someone out of the ordinary. What would they do under those circumstances?

There are several "If . . . then . . . ." prompts. Some of these will require copying two pages. The second page of these prompts (Then . . . .) is printed only once for purposes of saving space. You will be reminded to copy the second page when it might be necessary to the storyline.

Notice that children are given space for drawing pictures. Pictures are often an important part of the telling of these imaginative stories.

If I Had a Gorilla, Then...

In Mercer Mayer's *If I Had a Gorilla*, the main character wishes he had a gorilla (and any one of a number of other scary friends) so that he could prevent bigger kids or siblings from messing with him or his things.

Center discussion around problems with bullies or siblings. Ask students to imagine that they have a dragon or other kind of scary companion to protect them. Have them write about what would happen to them if they had such a friend to keep them from harm or bother. If appropriate, reproduce the "Then . . . " page, so that children might explain how their scary friend helps them in the same way that Mayer does in his book.

This prompt makes a humorous class book.

Daily Writing Prompts: **Fantasy**

Name _____ Date _____

If I had . . .

_____
_____
_____
_____
_____
_____
_____
_____
_____
_____

Name _____ **Date** _____

Then. . .

_____
_____
_____
_____
_____
_____
_____
_____
_____
_____
_____

Daily Writing Prompts: **Fantasy**

Daily Writing Prompts: **Fantasy**   **221**

If I Could Be a . . .

In James Howe's book *I Wish I Were a Butterfly*, a little cricket is not happy being a cricket. He wants to be a butterfly. He thinks he is ugly. When he hears the music made by another cricket, he is happy being who he is. There are numerous books and poems on the subject of wishing we were something or someone else. Select one to share before assigning the writing.

Ask children to draw who or what they might wish to be. Remind them that they might choose an animal or they might choose a person. Children might want to be Cinderella or Superman or a famous athlete. They might choose to be a butterfly or a snake or a dragon. Then ask them to write about becoming this character and what they would do.

REMINDER: Don't forget to reproduce the *Then* page (p. 220) if it is needed as a follow-up.

Daily Writing Prompts: **Fantasy**

Name _____ **Date** _____

If I could be . . .

_____
_____
_____
_____
_____
_____
_____
_____
_____
_____
_____

If I Had Wings

The words in the poem "Flying," by Josephine Van Dolen Pease (*Poetry Place Anthology*), make the idea of taking flight sound like fun! In the book *Red Balloon*, by Albert Lamorisse, a little boy is carried high over the city by a bunch of balloons. The idea of flying (without the help of a plane or helicopter) is a delightful one.

Prior to writing, center discussion around places one might go if he or she could grow wings. Ask children to write about what they would expect to see from their new viewpoint high in the sky. What is flying like?

REMINDER: Don't forget to reproduce the *Then* page, p. 220, if it is needed as a follow-up.

Name _____ **Date** _____

If I had wings . . .

If I Could Be the President

There are very few children who do not recognize the names of at least one or two of our past Presidents or the current office holder. *Arthur Meets the President*, by Marc Brown, gives us some idea of the high esteem we have for our country's leader.

Ask children to name some problems that they think might be handled by our President. If they could be the leader of our country, what would they do to help people? What do they imagine to be the job of the President? You will get a variety of responses depending upon the grade level you teach. This makes an interesting class book if you combine all responses and bind them together.

Name _____ **Date** _____

If I could be President . . .

Don't Bother Me! I'm Busy!

Spider does not want to be bothered while building a web in *The Very Busy Spider,* by Eric Carle. No one has time to listen to Andrew when he tries to tell about a bear in the house in *Nobody Listens to Andrew,* by Elizabeth Guilfoile. There are times when we don't want to be disturbed because we are busy doing something important to us.

Talk about things children like to do without interruptions. They might be too busy playing baseball to want to stop and eat lunch. They might be too busy watching their favorite cartoon to take time to clean their room. Have them write about a time they are "The Very Busy ____."

This prompt might also be written from the point of view of someone else. You might suggest the following:

> The Very Busy Teacher
> The Very Busy Mommy
> The Very Busy Daddy
> The Very Busy Caterpillar
> The Very Busy Tadpole

Daily Writing Prompts: **Fantasy**

Name _____ **Date** _____

The Very Busy _____

I'm Shrinking!

Your children may or may not have seen the movie *Honey, I Shrunk the Kids*. If they have seen it, they may be better able to imagine themselves as tiny creatures. If you were suddenly faced with the realization that you were the size of an ant, where could you go? What might happen to you?

In Chris Van Allsburg's book *Two Bad Ants*, we are given a story of fun and adventure from the ant's point of view. The illustrations help us imagine how big the world must look to a tiny creature.

Tell children that if they were the size of an ant they could crawl into small places, such as under closed doors in their house. Ask them to write about themselves as a tiny person the size of an ant. Have them answer where they will go, what they will see, if their family will miss them when they can't find them, and how they will get changed back into their normal size.

Wow! I'm as tiny as an ant! Now I can . . .

I'm a Giant!

This prompt proposes the opposite idea from the preceding one. Instead of being the size of an ant, have children imagine they are the size of a giant! Two books by Dav Pilkey (*Kat Kong* and *Dogzilla*) encourage us to imagine that common household pets might be gigantic creatures. Nearly everyone knows the story of Jack who met a giant at the top of his beanstalk. The illustrations of the giant's house help us realize how much bigger a house and furniture people might need if they were such a large size.

Ask children what they would do if they were the size of a giant. In Syd Hoff's *Danny and the Dinosaur,* the huge creature is kind and helpful. Ask children if they would also be kind. What could they do for their friends if they were the size of a giant? Have them write a story about what they can do now that they are giant. Encourage them also to tell how they managed to regain their normal size.

Name _____ Date _____

Oh, boy! I'm as big as a giant! Now I can . . .

My One Wish

There are many stories about wishes. Pauline Watson's *Wriggles the Little Wishing Pig* is a good example. Wriggles realizes that wishing to have features of other animals isn't such a good idea when he scares his uncle. *The Three Wishes,* a tale that has been retold by many different authors, is another good example of wishes gone bad. The woodsman is granted three wishes and manages to waste them.

Ask children to imagine they were granted just one wish. What might they do with that wish? What would they want? Would they share their good fortune? Have them write a story about their one wish.

Name _____ **Date** _____

I've been granted just **one** wish . . .

What's Behind the Door?

Ask children if they have ever wondered what was behind a closed door. The poem "Doors," by Jean Brabham McKinney (*Poetry Place Anthology*), reminds us of just how many kinds of doors there are in a house. Ask children what might happen if they opened a strange door. It might be a door to a room. It might be a cupboard or closet door. It might be a door to an underground cave! Have children write about opening a mysterious door and tell what they found on the other side.

Name _____ **Date** _____

I found a secret door. I opened it and . . .

I Ride Like the Wind on My Bike

After a busy day at school, it's sometimes nice to jump on a bike and ride like the wind. You don't need to be going anyplace special, just riding. You feel the wind in your face. You smell the fresh air and get a burst of energy. You feel as though you could go anywhere in the world. "My Bike," a poem by Bobbe Indgin (*Poetry Place Anthology*), helps us imagine the thrill of riding a bike: "The sidewalk's my highway . . . ." and I can go anywhere.

Ask children where they go when they get on their bikes and take a ride. Where would they like to go if they could go anywhere? What would they do there? What would they see? Have them write a story about a bike adventure.

Name _____ **Date** _____

When I get on my bike and ride like the wind, I . . .

A Magical School Bus Ride

When Miss Frizzle studies a special unit in her classroom, she takes her students for a ride on *The Magic School Bus* (a series by Joanna Cole and Bruce Degen). Using the format of the series, think of a science unit that you cover in your classroom. As a class or group, write your own version of a trip on a magical school bus. Where would you go and what would you see? Try to make this a nonfiction piece of writing.

An example might be to ride a magical bus to the zoo. Each child writes about a different animal. Or, ride a magical bus to the rain forest. Children write about animals and plants they find. When putting together a class book, pages can be combined in such a way that they represent the different layers of the rain forest (canopy, understory, etc.) or the different types of animals in the zoo (reptiles, amphibians, mammals, etc.).

Name _____ **Date** _____

Our class took a trip on a magical school bus to . . .

Daily Writing Prompts: **Fantasy**

It Would Be Silly If . . .

Audrey Wood wrote a book called *Silly Sally*. Sally meets many characters on her way to town. She tries to act like each character she meets along the way. Sally is a silly character as she walks backwards upside down.

There are lots of silly things in the minds of your children. Let their imaginations fly! What else would be silly? The prompt begins with the phrase "It would be silly if . . . ." Brainstorm a few ideas about silly things.

Once again you will notice a large space for an illustration. A picture of an owl putting on running shoes helps us imagine that ". . . It would be silly if an owl wore shoes. . . ." Collect this writing prompt and bind it to make a fun class book.

Name _____ **Date** _____

It would be silly if . . .

_____
_____
_____
_____
_____
_____
_____
_____

If the World Was All One Color

Share the following poem with children to initiate a discussion about the importance of having a world of many colors.

Colors

Imagine a world without color—
Where everything always looks gray.
No yellow sun or blue sky,
No rainbows to brighten our day.
Imagine a world without orange,
Or red or purple or blue.
I'm glad there's a world full of colors.
I'll bet you like colors too.

Have children imagine the world as all one color. Ask them what color they would choose. What problems could arise because of the situation? How would they change the world back to its normal colors? Have them write a story about what the world would be like if everything was the same color.

Name _____ **Date** _____

My world is all one color!

Daily Writing Prompts: **Fantasy**

When I Found My Lost . . .

Look for a version of the old story *The Mitten,* retold by Jan Brett or Alvin Tresselt, for example. The child in the story loses a mitten in the snow. Many animals make a new home together inside the mitten. The child finds the mitten and tries to imagine what happened that caused it to burst at the seams.

Ask children to imagine that they have lost a mitten, hat, scarf, or boot in the snow. Have them write a story about what happens to the lost item. Where and how did they lose it? Does an animal move in? Does another child find it and use it? Remind them not to forget to write an ending to the story. How do they get the lost item back and what was its condition? How did it get ripped or unraveled?

Daily Writing Prompts: **Fantasy**

Name _____ **Date** _____

I was playing in the snow and I lost my . . .

My Mixed-Up Animal

Eric Carle wrote a book about a chameleon who wished it had some characteristics of other creatures in nature. The chameleon ended up looking like a silly but scary character who finally wishes himself back to normal. In *The Mixed-Up Chameleon* you will find wonderful illustrations to accompany the story. The chameleon becomes more and more strange looking as it adds parts of other animals to its own body.

Ask children to select two real animals to put together into a single creature. One might combine an elephant and a giraffe. The resulting animal might have a trunk and a very long neck. There is a large space for a picture as this will be an important part of the assignment. Lines are provided for writing a description of the mixed-up animal. This would also make a good book.

248 Daily Writing Prompts: **Fantasy**

Name _____ **Date** _____

My mixed-up animal is made out of _____

_____

_____

_____

_____

_____

_____

_____

_____

You'll Know My House Because . . .

Daniel Pinkwater's book *The Big Orange Splot* tells the engaging story of Mr. Plumbean, who changes the looks of his house after a bird drops a large splot of orange paint on his roof. All of the houses on his block look the same and the people like it that way. One by one the neighbors come to tell Mr. Plumbean that he should not have made the changes to his house. One by one they go home and make changes to their own houses. Share this book before using the writing and drawing prompt that follows.

Have children imagine that the houses on their block look the same. Ask how they would make their house look different. Mr. Plumbean's house looks like his dreams. How will their house show their dreams? Have them draw and describe their dream house.

Name _____ **Date** _____

You will know which house belongs to me because . . .

_____
_____
_____
_____
_____
_____
_____

Daily Writing Prompts: **Fantasy**

What Can You Do with a Box?

Children delight in playing with empty boxes. Whenever a family gets a new refrigerator, washing machine, air conditioner, or window fan, the box in which it arrives can become a great toy for someone with imagination.

Share Patricia Lee Gauch's book *Christina Katerina and the Box*. This book will surely inspire a discussion of things you can do with a big box. Ask children to write a story from their own experiences with box palaces, box race cars, and the like. Boxes can be fun! If they have not had the opportunity to play with a big box, ask them to imagine what they would make from one and then write about that.

Name _____ **Date** _____

I had lots of fun playing with a big box.

_____
_____
_____
_____
_____
_____
_____
_____
_____
_____
_____
_____
_____
_____
_____
_____
_____
_____
_____
_____

My Pet Dinosaur

The little boy in Syd Hoff's book *Danny and the Dinosaur* has a great time playing with his huge animal friend. The dinosaur plays nicely with all of the children and helps them do all kinds of things. Ask children to imagine they have a pet dinosaur. What might they do with their dinosaur? Would there be a problem if they had such a large pet? Where would they keep it? How would they feed it and keep it clean? Have them write a story about themselves and their pet.

Name _____ **Date** _____

I have a lot of fun with my pet dinosaur.

_____
_____
_____
_____
_____
_____
_____
_____
_____
_____
_____
_____
_____
_____
_____
_____
_____
_____
_____
_____
_____
_____
_____

How Some Animals REALLY Work

Alan Snow has written a book about the inner workings of a common household pet. *How Dogs Really Work* is a whimsical look at the numerous mechanisms one might imagine inside of a dog that would make it do the things dogs do. Share this book before using the prompt because the illustrations will help children understand the idea behind it. This prompt is probably most appropriate for third-graders and up. The humor is a bit more sophisticated than that in other animal books.

Allow groups of children to work together to describe imaginative working parts that might be found on some common animals. Group pages together to make small books that can be shared with others. Some ideas for group books might be the following:

> How Cats Really Work
> How Birds Really Work
> How Fish Really Work

By allowing children to work in small groups on specific animals, you will probably find that the resulting stories are more imaginative. Each group member could write about a specific part of the animal.

Name _____ **Date** _____

This is how a _____ really works.

_____
_____
_____
_____
_____
_____
_____
_____
_____

My Food Talked to Me

Anansi is a tricky spider from African tales. In Eric Kimmel's retelling of *Anansi & the Talking Melon,* the spider crawls inside a melon and gets stuck. When Elephant picks up the melon, Anansi talks. Elephant thinks the melon must be magic because it speaks to him. It causes problems when the King doesn't believe Elephant has a magic melon.

Have children imagine that a piece of food could talk to them. What would it say? What kind of food would they want to have speak to them? Have them select a food and then write a story about it.

Name _____ **Date** _____

I just heard my _____ talking to me!

Look at Me! I'm Flat as a Pancake!

In Jeff Brown's *Flat Stanley*, Stanley Lambchop becomes flat when a bulletin board falls on him. He is able to do brave and dangerous deeds because of his new flat condition. There is a bit of jealousy from a sibling because of the attention Stanley gets.

Have children imagine they have a condition like Stanley Lambchop. Ask them what they would be able to do if they were flat like a pancake. Have them write a story about this.

Daily Writing Prompts: **Fantasy**

Name _____ **Date** _____

I'm flat as a pancake! Now I can . . .

Miscellaneous Writing Prompts

This large section of writing prompts contains a variety of ways to respond to literature and poetry. You will find a variety of genres being suggested. You will find suggestions that lead to changing the ending or adding to the ending of a specific story. You will find parodies of alphabet and number books and poems. Children will be asked to predict a story after being given words and phrases from the text or they will be given a wordless picture book to add text to. There are directions for making reversible books and peephole books. Depending upon the selection, the resulting work might be a postcard, a list, or a story.

You will note that not all prompts in this section have an accompanying reproducible page. Instead, you will find a detailed description telling how to produce an unusual piece of writing. Give these ideas a try. The results are really quite fun! It is hoped that you will refer often to the many ideas in this section.

I Went Walking...

You will find multiple pages with this prompt because it can be used in writing about many kinds of walks. The book *I Went Walking,* by Sue Williams, contains a specific pattern that emergent readers might be asked to parody. You will find a page with that simple prompt. The blank spaces require insertion of a color word and an animal name (example: I went walking. I saw a brown lizard following me). You might want to combine all pages in a class book. Use the space at the top of the page for colorful illustrations.

You will also find prompts that offer opportunities to write about taking a walk through the rain forest, the woods, down the street, and other places. Use these prompts as nonfiction assignments when possible. If you have just finished a unit on the rain forest or the sea you might wish to have children write what they would see if they visited that place. Select your accompanying materials from your nonfiction library. A final prompt in this section asks for a description not from a walk but from a dive into the sea.

Miscellaneous Writing Prompts

Name _____ **Date** _____

I went walking. I saw a _____

_____ following me.

Miscellaneous Writing Prompts

Name _____ **Date** _____

I went walking in the rain forest. I saw . . .

_____
_____
_____
_____
_____
_____
_____
_____
_____
_____

Name _____ Date _____

I went walking in the sand. I saw . . .

_____
_____
_____
_____
_____
_____
_____
_____
_____
_____

Name _____ **Date** _____

I went walking on the farm. I saw . . .

_____
_____
_____
_____
_____
_____
_____
_____
_____
_____

Name _____ **Date** _____

I went walking through the woods. I saw . . .

_____
_____
_____
_____
_____
_____
_____
_____
_____
_____

Miscellaneous Writing Prompts

From *Daily Writing Prompts*. Text © Carol Simpson and illustrations © Good Year Books.

Name _____ **Date** _____

I went walking in my house. I saw . . .

_____
_____
_____
_____
_____
_____
_____
_____
_____
_____

Name _____ Date _____

I went walking in my school. I saw . . .

_____
_____
_____
_____
_____
_____
_____
_____
_____

Name _____   **Date** _____

I went walking down my street. I saw . . .

_____
_____
_____
_____
_____
_____
_____
_____
_____

Name _____ Date _____

I went diving in the sea. I saw . . .

_____
_____
_____
_____
_____
_____
_____
_____
_____
_____

My Week

Cindy Ward has written a book entitled *Cookie's Week.* Children delight in the antics of Cookie, a cat. Each day of the week the cat does something to get into trouble. Cookie knocks over a flowerpot and she climbs on the curtains, to name but two of her antics. When Sunday comes ". . . maybe Cookie will rest. . . ." but we see a slightly open eye and we know better.

This prompt asks children to write something for each of the seven days in a week. It could be a story about the individual child's week or the week of a fictitious character. The story evolves around something that happens each day. The finished product may resemble a diary. Begin the writing on a Monday. Remember to add to the story each day that week. After having written something for each of the five days of the school week, children can take their papers home and finish their writing during the weekend as homework!

Select several good examples of this writing assignment and type them on the computer, allowing a page for each day of the week. The children who have written the selected stories can then illustrate each day and make a book out of their adventures for a week.

Miscellaneous Writing Prompts **273**

Name _____ Date _____

_____ Week

On Monday _____
_____
_____

On Tuesday _____
_____
_____

On Wednesday _____
_____
_____

On Thursday _____
_____
_____

On Friday _____
_____
_____

On Saturday _____
_____
_____

On Sunday _____
_____
_____

274   Miscellaneous Writing Prompts

From *Daily Writing Prompts*. Text © Carol Simpson and illustrations © Good Year Books.

A Dark Tale

Ruth Brown's book *A Dark Dark Tale* is the familiar story of the dark dark house with the dark dark stairs and the dark dark room. Have children write their own dark tale following this pattern. The story should end with something in a box. Discuss places in the house where the story might lead. Although the basic pattern requires filling in blanks, it will still allow for creativity. If you wish to change the basic pattern to "behind that dark dark . . . " or up the dark dark . . . ", you may do so by asking children to copy phrases from the board or chart paper rather than using the reproducible page.

A second prompt page allows for an open-ended narrative about a scary place or event. For some children, this format might be easier than the pattern page.

Miscellaneous Writing Prompts

My Dark Dark Tale

In the dark dark _____

      there was a dark dark _____.

In the dark dark _____

      there was a dark dark _____.

In the dark dark _____

      there was a dark dark _____.

In the dark dark _____

      there was a dark dark _____.

In the dark dark _____

      there was a dark dark box.

And in that dark dark box there was a

_____.

Name _____ **Date** _____

My Dark Dark Tale

This Is Me!

Have children describe themselves using adjectives, following the basic pattern of the poem below, which has two adjectives per line. You may not want to require that words rhyme as they do here.

Me

This is me:
    happy, glad
    angry, mad
    playful, wild
    lazy, mild
    noisy, loud
    quiet, proud
    helpful, caring
    kind, sharing
    curious, free
    most of all . . .
    Glad to be
    ME!

Miscellaneous Writing Prompts

Name _____ Date _____

Me

This is me:

_____ , _____

_____ , _____

_____ , _____

_____ , _____

_____ , _____

_____ , _____

_____ , _____

curious, free

most of all . . .

Glad to be

ME!

Compare Yourself to an Animal

Audrey Wood's book *Quick As a Cricket* is filled with comparisons of human and animal characteristics. Each page contains the basic pattern sentence . . .

"I'm as _____ as a _____."

Two adjacent pages present opposite ideas. "I'm as noisy as a . . . ." followed by "I'm as quiet as a . . . ." The descriptive phrases compare the character to an animal. For example, "I'm as noisy as a parrot," "I'm as quiet as a mouse."

Emergent readers might be asked to fill only one of the prompt pages to describe themselves. Second-graders might be asked to complete two pages using opposite pairs of words (hot/cold, noisy/quiet, nice/mean, etc.). You might ask third-graders and up to complete a set of prompt pages, such as four sets of opposite pairs.

Name _____ **Date** _____

I'm as _____ as a _____ .

Miscellaneous Writing Prompts

Dear Zoo, Please Send Me a Pet

Emergent readers enjoy writing a page of a class book that parodies Rod Campbell's *Dear Zoo*. In the book, a child writes a letter to the zoo asking them to send a pet. Each time the pet is sent back to the zoo because it is too tall or too grumpy or too scary. Finally the zoo sends an animal that is just right. So the child decides to keep him.

If you combine your children's prompts into a class book, be sure to write an introductory page that explains the idea behind the book. For example, write a letter to the zoo, similar to the one in Rod Campbell's book. Children do their part by filling in the blanks on the prompt page. The final page in the class book should be the name of the pet that is just right so we keep it and an illustration of it.

Name _____ **Date** _____

The zoo sent me a _____ .

But, _____

_____

so I sent it back!

A Story About Opposites

That's Good! That's Bad!, by Margery Cuyler, is the story of a boy who gets carried off by a large balloon his parents buy for him. His adventure repeats the pattern of things going from good to bad to good again. Fortunately, by Remy Charlip, is another example of a story that goes from good to bad to good again. Have children follow the pattern of these two books by writing at least five events that go from good to bad, back and forth, and end with something good.

Younger students might be asked to write a simpler story with only three events that go from good to bad and end with something good. An example might be the following. (Note the three parts as they are shown in varying fonts.)

I went to my friend's birthday party. We had cake and ice cream and played games. I won a prize! *When I opened it, a mouse jumped out and scared me. I screamed and dropped the box.* The mouse was cute and cuddly. I took it home and made a cage for it. Now it's my pet.

284   Miscellaneous Writing Prompts

Name _____ Date _____

My Good and Bad Adventure

I've Got Antlers!

Imogene has a big problem. She grows antlers on her head. Her antlers get used by members of her family for many things, including a clothes rack. Poor Imogene. Share *Imogene's Antlers,* by David Small. Ask children what they would do if their bodies became covered in feathers. What if they grew a tail like a monkey? What if their ears grew to the size of a donkey's? Ask them to imagine having an elephant's trunk instead of a nose. Discuss fantastic ideas such as these in preparation for the writing prompt on the next page. You might also want to have them write about getting rid of their problem, if they can.

Name _____ **Date** _____

You won't believe this, but I've got _____!

Retell a Fairy Tale

If you search the shelves in your library, you will probably find an example of a fairy tale rewrite. Marilyn Tolhurst's *Somebody and the Three Blairs,* Ellen Jackson's *Cinder Edna,* and Jon Scieszka's *The True Story of the Three Little Pigs* are several examples. Children delight in hearing these unique "other" versions and enjoy arguing for one side of the story or the other.

After sharing a selection of stories, or at least two with opposing ideas based upon a single fairy tale, ask children to write a paragraph defending their belief of which story is "true." Children need to be sure to tell why they have their particular belief. If need be, suggest that they defend their stand by presenting a specified number of supporting details. You might even wish to have a "trial" in the classroom. Proponents of each side can get up and debate their opinions. In the end, the fairy tale character can be voted guilty or innocent. This prompt offers a good opportunity to write a persuasive paper.

Name _____ **Date** _____

Here is what I believe is the real story of _____
_____!

Teddy Bear, Teddy Bear

Using the pattern of the familiar rhyme, "Teddy Bear, Teddy Bear," writers will complete a sentence by filling in a verb phrase. Michael Hague has done a cute version of the poem in book form.

Teddy Bear might do the following and more:

> *Teddy Bear, Teddy Bear, touch your toe . . . tie your shoe . . . run a race . . . jump up and down . . . say the Pledge . . . sit on a chair . . . go to sleep . . . eat your supper . . . .*

There is space for an accompanying illustration for the prompt. This one is especially suitable for emergent readers who would be asked to complete just one page each. The pages could then be bound into a class book. It would not be necessary to try to rhyme the pages.

Ask older children to write an entire eight- to twelve-line version of the poem, complete with rhyming words. Supply them with enough copies of the prompt page to complete the assignment. Put their verses together in individual books to share with younger children, especially kindergartners, who are usually familiar with the poem.

Miscellaneous Writing Prompts

Name _____ **Date** _____

Teddy Bear, Teddy Bear _____

_____ .

Miscellaneous Writing Prompts **291**

I've Traveled This Land

My Sister's Rusty Bike is a delightful rhythmic pattern book by Jim Aylesworth. The boy in the book visits some of the 50 states and sees some interesting sights along the way. Depending upon the age and ability of your children, the pattern could be parodied. But you might also ask children to write a descriptive paragraph about a place of their choosing in their town or location. You will find prompts for either option.

Here's a sample parody based on the pattern of Aylesworth's book.

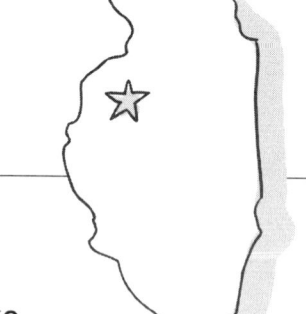

I rode to Illinois
On my sister's rusty bike,
And found just south of Galesburg
A place I think you'll like.
A guy lives there named Slim McFee.
His turkeys can't be beat.
His house is small but he doesn't mind.
It's easier to keep it neat.

Name _____ **Date** _____

My Bike Ride

I rode to _____

On my sister's rusty bike,

And found just _____ of _____

A place I think you'll like.

_____
_____
_____
_____
_____
_____
_____
_____
_____
_____
_____
_____
_____
_____
_____

Miscellaneous Writing Prompts

Name _____ **Date** _____

One of my favorite local places to visit is . . .

Predict the Story of Little Grunt

In *Little Grunt and the Big Egg,* by Tomie dePaola, Little Grunt lives in a cave with his pet dinosaur. His family realizes that having a huge dinosaur for a pet is a big problem. The dinosaur has to go! But when the cave family is threatened by a volcano, the dinosaur returns to save the day.

The prompt for this assignment is a listing of words and phrases taken from the story, in order of their appearance. Before you share the featured book, share the introduction above and then copy and distribute the words and phrases on the next page. Ask children to guess the story by writing their own version. They should use all (or close to all) of the prompts in their story. Share them before and/or after reading the real story.

Miscellaneous Writing Prompts   **295**

Name _____ Date _____

Predict the Story!

1. in a big cave
2. Little Grunt
3. biggest egg ever seen
4. pulled it home
5. egg broke
6. baby dinosaur
7. began to grow
8. still hungry
9. play rough
10. The giant lizard GOES!
11. volcano
12. came to save us

Make a Peep Hole Book

This writing idea does not contain a reproducible page with it. You will be determining just how much writing is required in response to the assignment.

Allow children to look in science magazines to find large pictures of various animals. Each child selects just one picture and glues it to a sheet of heavy construction or drawing paper.

Collect all the mounted pictures. You will be putting them together to make a book using either metal rings or a spiral binding machine. Before you bind the pages, place a blank sheet of heavy paper in front of each of the animal pages to serve as your peep hole page. Next, using a sharp cutting tool, carefully cut a hole in the sheet of heavy paper that is placed in front of each animal page. Cut the hole so that it exposes a small part of the animal picture that appears on the next page. You might want to cut the hole so that it exposes just an eye or a nose or a tail. It is best if the teacher does the cutting.

The peep hole page is also the writing page. If you work with emergent readers and want children to learn each other's names, you can write the words "Guess what _____ saw?" on each page. The blank is for the child to write his or her name. Share the "Guess what . . . " pages, point out the small exposed part of the animal, and let children try to guess what the animal might be. This makes a great guessing book. If your children are able to write a description, ask them to

Miscellaneous Writing Prompts **297**

write about the animal they chose but without giving its name. Have them write their description on the empty page with the hole cut in it. After everyone has written their description, share them and let children guess the animal on the next page. Again, another great guessing book.

If you need an example of a peep hole book, look for *Whose Toes Are Those? A Peep Hole Story,* by Joyce Elias. It contains poems that describe the animals we are asked to guess. And the hole exposes only feet! Children love to guess whose feet they are seeing. Another example of a peep hole story is *Who's in the Shed?,* by Brenda Parkes. In this story, farm animals try to figure out what animal is in the barn. They can only see parts of the animal through the holes.

Use Your Senses to Describe Something

The poem "Smells," by Kathryn Worth (*Random House Book of Poetry for Children*), talks about the smells that fill the air in springtime. The sense of smell is only one of the senses we use every day. The prompts that follow ask children to describe each of the four seasons using all five of their senses.

Before writing, talk about the things children see, hear, smell, taste, and touch in the season they are going to describe. You may want to find other poems that are appropriate for fall, winter, and summer.

There is a generic prompt page that could be used to describe many different settings. For example, ask children to describe a garden, the sea, or their kitchen on Thanksgiving morning, to name but a few.

Miscellaneous Writing Prompts

Name _____ Date _____

Autumn

See

_____

_____

Hear

_____

_____

Touch

_____

_____

Taste

_____

_____

Smell

_____

_____

Name _____ Date _____

Winter

See
_____
_____

Hear
_____
_____

Touch
_____
_____

Taste
_____
_____

Smell
_____
_____

Name _____ Date _____

Spring

See

_____

_____

Hear

_____

_____

Touch

_____

_____

Taste

_____

_____

Smell

_____

_____

Name _____ Date _____

Summer

See
_____
_____

Hear
_____
_____

Touch
_____
_____

Taste
_____
_____

Smell
_____
_____

Name _____ Date _____

Describe a _____ .

See
_____
_____

Hear
_____
_____

Touch
_____
_____

Taste
_____
_____

Smell
_____
_____

Parody a Familiar Song

At the Christmas holiday, Christians might sing the song of "The Twelve Days of Christmas." It is a familiar tune and one that has been parodied. Examples are Carol Greene's *The Thirteen Days of Halloween*, Seymour Chwast's *Twelve Circus Rings*, and Wright Group's *Nine Days of Camping*.

This format can be used to describe, among other ideas, the following:

> The Twelve Days of Thanksgiving
> The Twelve Days of Autumn
> The Twelve Days of Winter
> The Twelve Days of Spring
> The Twelve Days of Summer
> The Twelve Days of Vacation

It is not necessary to repeat all of the previous days when adding something new each time, as the song does. Also, you may or may not want to require that there be three things on the third day, eleven things on the eleventh day, and so on. Just thinking of twelve ideas (or six ideas for a shorter version) on a specific subject may be sufficient.

Name _____ Date _____

The _____ Days of _____

On the first day _____
_____
_____

On the second day _____
_____
_____

On the third day _____
_____
_____

On the fourth day _____
_____
_____

On the fifth day _____
_____
_____

On the sixth day _____
_____
_____

Name _____ Date _____

The _____ Days of _____
(continued)

On the seventh day _____
_____
_____

On the eighth day _____
_____
_____

On the ninth day _____
_____
_____

On the tenth day _____
_____
_____

On the eleventh day _____
_____
_____

On the twelfth day _____
_____
_____

Miscellaneous Writing Prompts

Make a Reversible Book

You will not find a reproducible page with this writing idea. It is hoped that the description is complete enough that you will give it a try, and often. The reversible book is not difficult to make, and it results in a favorite writing activity.

Reversible books are based upon words that are opposites. One story is positive, and the other one negative. Among the numerous writing topics you might select are:

> Good Manners vs. Bad Manners
>
> Foods I Like vs. Foods I Don't Like
>
> The Good Wolf (or other animal) vs. The Bad Wolf

Begin the project by folding and center stapling two sheets of plain paper together, preferably 11" x 17" paper. The folded/stapled pages become a booklet. With staples on the left side, just as the seam on a real book would be, have children design a cover on the front page. Then have them write a three-page story by opening the pages of the booklet and keeping to the right side of the staples at all times. When they have finished their last page, direct them to close the booklet, flip the booklet upside down, leaving the staples on the left side once again. They will see that there is another blank "front page" and three follow-up pages inside! There they can write their next story.

308   Miscellaneous Writing Prompts

Reversible books are appropriate for younger as well as older children. The subject matter will vary, and the length of the reversible books might vary also. Be sure to allow time to illustrate these reversible books. Children enjoy sharing the books with younger classes.

Write a Letter to a Fairy Tale Character

Janet and Allan Ahlberg have written books that contain letters or postcards that can be pulled out of pockets and envelopes. *The Jolly Postman or Other People's Letters* and *Jolly Christmas Postman* are both fun books to read to children.

Have children select a favorite fairy tale character and write them a letter. Someone writing to Goldilocks might want to tell her that it is not a good idea to go inside a stranger's house. The Prince in the story of the Frog Prince might need a bit of advice on how to charm the Princess into kissing him and releasing him from a spell.

The prompt is designed for writing a letter. It is generic and might be used for another letter-writing project as well.

Dear _____ ,

I just wanted you to know that . . .

_____
_____
_____
_____
_____
_____
_____
_____
_____
_____
_____
_____
_____
_____
_____
_____
_____
_____

Sincerely,

_____

Miscellaneous Writing Prompts

An Hour By Hour Story

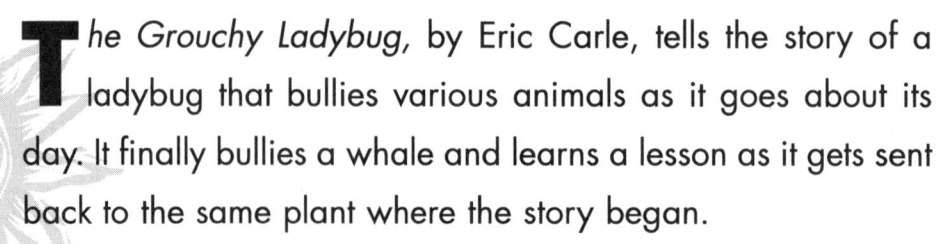

The Grouchy Ladybug, by Eric Carle, tells the story of a ladybug that bullies various animals as it goes about its day. It finally bullies a whale and learns a lesson as it gets sent back to the same plant where the story began.

Have children select a character (person, animal, bug, etc.) and write what happens hour by hour as the character goes about its day. The character might be a spider in search of a fly. It might be a child in search of a friend. It might be a bear looking for a cave. Each hour of the day another problem occurs so the search must continue until 12:00 when things are just right.

Name _____ **Date** _____

At 1:00 _____

At 2:00 _____

At 3:00 _____

At 4:00 _____

At 5:00 _____

At 6:00 _____

At 7:00 _____

At 8:00 _____

At 9:00 _____

At 10:00 _____

At 11:00 _____

At 12:00 _____

And _____ was happy at last.

Miscellaneous Writing Prompts

Create a Story Based on a Picture

Have children choose a picture from a magazine that shows action, activity, or emotion. After they study the picture, have them write a story based upon what they see. You may preselect a single picture and reproduce it for each child if you don't have time to let each child select his or her own.

A variation on this idea is to choose an unfamiliar story from a basal, reproduce at least four of the pictures that demonstrate the sequence of the actual story, and then paste them on the pages of a folded stapled booklet, one picture per page. Put writing lines on the bottom of each page and reproduce sets of the blank storybooks for children. Have them write the story they think is represented by the sequence of pictures. After sharing their stories, you might wish to read aloud the actual story from the basal.

Describe a Face

Use the following poem as the starting point for a discussion of "reading" faces.

Moods

I smile when I'm happy.
I cry when I'm sad.
I grin when I'm silly,
And I frown when I'm mad.
Look at my face
And you can see
The way that I'm feeling
Inside of me.

Select a picture from a magazine that shows emotion. Glue it to a sheet of paper and put writing lines at the bottom. Reproduce a copy for each child. Ask children to write a story based upon the smile, frown, or other look on the face of the person in the picture. Why is that person feeling the way they are feeling? What happened to them?

Miscellaneous Writing Prompts

A Postcard from Camp

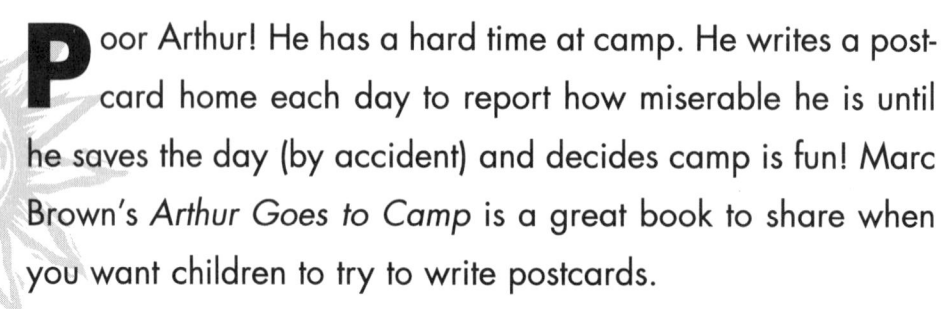

Poor Arthur! He has a hard time at camp. He writes a postcard home each day to report how miserable he is until he saves the day (by accident) and decides camp is fun! Marc Brown's *Arthur Goes to Camp* is a great book to share when you want children to try to write postcards.

Lynn Cherry's *The Armadillo from Amarillo* is also a good example for presenting postcard writing. The armadillo travels around the United States on the wings of an eagle. He is always sending postcards to his cousin. He tells about the places he sees during his travels.

Have children use the generic postcard prompt on the next page to write their own postcards. The postcards might be written about a place visited during a vacation, to describe the ocean or the rain forest or another place that was studied in a science unit, or from a place they would like to go to.

The empty box is for the child to draw the picture that is usually found on the front of a postcard. Have children address their postcard in the appropriate place to someone back home.

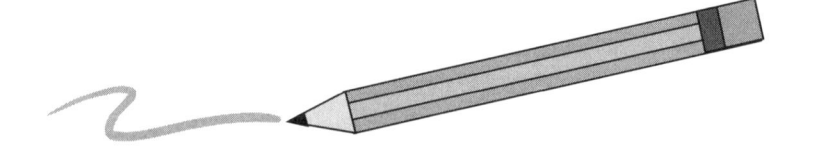

Miscellaneous Writing Prompts

Name _____   Date _____

To:

Love, _____

Miscellaneous Writing Prompts   317

Alphabetical Listing

There are numerous books written in an A-B-C format. Jerry Pallotta's many A-B-C books contain page after page of factual information about furry animals, butterflies, icky bugs, and more. If you want children to include factual information in their A-B-C books, Pallotta's books should be closely examined for ideas.

Among the A-B-C books is another one of particular interest. *Oliver's Alphabets,* by Lisa Bruce, has an alphabetical listing with each picture. A playground picture has a list of words from *a* to *z* to accompany the illustration. A zoo picture would have its own list from *a* to *z* as well. Students can look at the variety of listings to get ideas for their own subject matter.

Depending upon the age and ability of your children, you may want to vary the prompt requirements. You may ask them to simply list something for each letter. You might ask them to write a fact about each of their items. Or you might want them to write using only a small segment of the alphabet. Emergent writers could be asked to use only seven letters, selected in order (example: *c* to *i* or *m* to *s*). Filling in all letters can be difficult, especially letters *q* and *x*.

Miscellaneous Writing Prompts

Name _____ **Date** _____

The _____ A-B-Cs

A _____ N _____

B _____ O _____

C _____ P _____

D _____ Q _____

E _____ R _____

F _____ S _____

G _____ T _____

H _____ U _____

I _____ V _____

J _____ W _____

K _____ X _____

L _____ Y _____

M _____ Z _____

A Number Story

Seven Little Monsters, by Maurice Sendak, is only one of many stories written in a number pattern. Sendak's book goes up to seven, with each of the seven little monsters doing or saying something different. "Five Big Whales" (Anonymous) and "Five Baby Birds" (Anonymous) both go up to the number five. The poem "10 Little Caterpillars," by Bill Martin, Jr., goes up to ten. Using these patterns as a model, have children write their own story using the prompt page(s) that follow. You should determine how far the children should be expected to write.

To allow for flexibility, you will see that number word prompts and ordinal prompts are provided for your choosing. By reproducing only one page, your stories can stop at five rather than at ten.

Name _____ **Date** _____

One
_____
_____
_____

Two
_____
_____
_____

Three
_____
_____
_____

Four
_____
_____
_____

Five
_____
_____
_____

Miscellaneous Writing Prompts

Six

Seven

Eight

Nine

Ten

Name _____ **Date** _____

The first one
_____
_____
_____

The second one
_____
_____
_____

The third one
_____
_____
_____

The fourth one
_____
_____
_____

The fifth one
_____
_____
_____

Miscellaneous Writing Prompts

The sixth one

_____
_____
_____

The seventh one

_____
_____
_____

The eighth one

_____
_____
_____

The ninth one

_____
_____
_____

The tenth one

_____
_____
_____

A Number Story in Reverse

Share the poem below as an example of writing that uses numbers in descending order. You might also share *Ten in a Bed,* by Allan Ahlberg. Have children write their own poem using this style. You should determine whether children should start with "Five" or "Ten." You also should decide whether or not to require rhyme in your children's work.

Five Fuzzy Spiders

Five fuzzy spiders crawling up the door,
One slipped and broke a leg, then there were four.
Four fuzzy spiders climbing in a tree,
One stubbed his little toe, then there were three.
Three fuzzy spiders hiding in a shoe,
One got stepped on, then there were two.
Two fuzzy spiders looking for some fun,
One got a tummyache, then there was one.
One fuzzy spider resting in the sun,
Along came a hungry bird, then there were none!

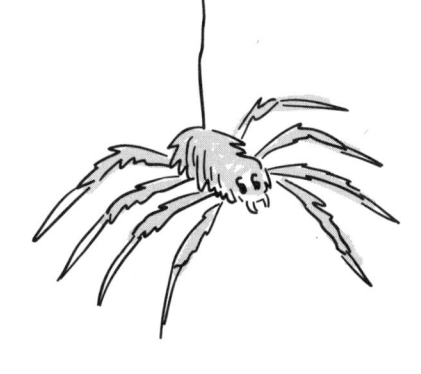

Miscellaneous Writing Prompts

Name _____ Date _____

Ten
_____
_____
_____

Nine
_____
_____
_____

Eight
_____
_____
_____

Seven
_____
_____
_____

Six
_____
_____
_____

Name _____ **Date** _____

Five
_____
_____
_____

Four
_____
_____
_____

Three
_____
_____
_____

Two
_____
_____
_____

One
_____
_____
_____

Add a Character to a Pirate Story

If you look at Mem Fox's book *Tough Boris*, you will notice that the words in the story only mention the pirate. If you look closely at the illustrations you will note that a little boy is also an important character in the story.

Using the prompt on the following page, have children write a story about that little boy. Have them transfer their story onto sticky notes and place the words of the story directly upon the pages of the book. When the little boy or the pirate is speaking directly, place sticky notes in the shape of a bubble above the person's head.

The prompt might also be used as a title for a generic pirate adventure, or as a culminating writing activity after sharing the chapter book *Pearl's Pirates*, by Frank Asch.

Name _____ **Date** _____

The Pirate Ship Adventure

Add a Character to the Barnyard

Rosie's Walk, by Pat Hutchins, is an example of a picture book that has a character that is never mentioned in the text. The story of Rosie the hen is told in the words, but the fox is never mentioned. Rosie is followed around the barnyard by the fox, who has a lot of trouble trying to catch the little hen for lunch! A child-written "The Fox's Walk" makes a great story. Have children use the book's illustrations to help them write a story about this secondary character.

Another option is to transfer the text of "The Fox's Walk" onto sticky notes and place them directly on the pages of the book. If the fox is speaking, show what the fox said by cutting the sticky note in the shape of a speech bubble and pasting it above the fox's head.

Miscellaneous Writing Prompts

Name _____ Date _____

The Fox's Walk

A Letter to Mother Earth

The prompt that follows is a letter to Mother Earth. Schim Schimmel has written and illustrated a beautiful book entitled *Dear Children of the Earth*. This book is a letter from Mother Earth to us. Mother Earth asks us to take care of the Earth and the animals. We are reminded that we share a single valuable (but vulnerable) home and we should protect it from harm. Have children write a letter back to Mother Earth telling her what we can do to help protect our home.

Dear Mother Earth,

_____

_____

_____

_____

_____

_____

_____

_____

_____

_____

_____

_____

_____

_____

_____

_____

_____

Love,
_____

Create a Travel Brochure

Bring in travel brochures from your local travel agency. Allow children to study them to see how they are put together. The easiest examples to try to parody are those that are tri-fold designs. Ask children to design a tri-fold brochure that tells about a place they have visited. If children have not traveled to other places, let them write a brochure about a local attraction or a place they might like to visit someday. If you have just finished a science or social studies unit that can be depicted in a brochure, let this activity become an assessment tool.

There is no prompt page to reproduce. It is suggested that you use plain 8-1/2" x 11" paper, folded in thirds. You determine how many of the resulting six sections children are expected to fill with information and drawings.

Miscellaneous Writing Prompts

Finish the Story of an Alligator

The story of *An Alligator Named . . . Alligator*, by Lois Grambling, is about a boy named Elmo who has a pet alligator. The alligator causes problems and has to be sent to the zoo. The story ends with Elmo finding two eggs sitting on his pillow. Have children read the story of Elmo before you ask them to continue the story by writing what happens to the two eggs. Ask them if the eggs are alligator eggs. Does Elmo decide to tell anyone about the eggs? Can Elmo keep another pet alligator or two a secret?

Name _____ Date _____

When Elmo found two eggs on his pillow, he decided to . . .

Finish the Story of Anansi

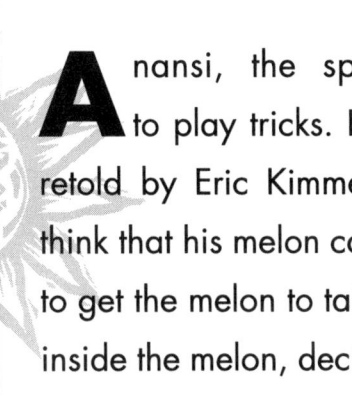

Anansi, the spider in several African tales, loves to play tricks. In the book *Anansi & the Talking Melon*, retold by Eric Kimmel, the tricky spider makes an elephant think that his melon can talk. Trouble arises when the King tries to get the melon to talk and it doesn't, because Anansi, who is inside the melon, decides not to say anything. At the end of the story, the elephant thinks that his bananas can talk.

Share the story of Anansi before doing the writing prompt on the next page. Ask children to continue the story by telling what the elephant does with his talking bananas. Does Anansi climb into yet another one of Elephant's garden plants and play another trick on him?

Name _____ Date _____

Elephant thought that his bananas could talk so he . . .

_____
_____
_____
_____
_____
_____
_____
_____
_____
_____
_____
_____
_____
_____
_____
_____
_____
_____
_____
_____
_____

Finish the Story of Grandpa and His Slippers

Read aloud *Grandpa's Slippers*, by Joy Watson, so children can hear and enjoy the delightful pattern in the words. Grandpa does not want to part with his slippers even though they have holes and the soles are worn out. When his slippers finally fall apart in his hands, he has to consent to wearing the new pair that Grandma bought for him earlier in the story. At the end of the story Grandma tells Grandpa that he now needs a new cardigan.

Using the repetitive pattern in the book as a model, have children write a new version of the story, telling what happens each day because Grandpa does not want to part with his old cardigan. The story could actually continue beyond that, with Grandma telling him he needs new socks or a new hat! The possibilities are endless.

Name _____ Date _____

Grandpa doesn't want Grandma to get rid of his old cardigan so he . . .

Finish the Story of Being Followed Home

When Robert is followed home by a whole herd of hippos, it causes many problems for his family. Margaret Mahy's *The Boy Who Was Followed Home* is a delightful story about a boy who loves animals. As the number of hippos in the family's yard increases, the desire to get rid of them gets stronger. Father resorts to tricks. However, when the hippos are gone, along come some giraffes to take their place! Have children continue the story by writing about how Robert would get rid of the giraffes. Children might also choose yet another animal to follow Robert home at the end of their stories.

Name _____ **Date** _____

Robert's family doesn't like the giraffes that followed him home so . . .

Predict the Story of Choco

Using words and phrases taken from the book *A Mother for Choco,* by Keiko Kasza, ask children to try to predict what they think will happen in the story and write about it. Choco, a little bird, can't find his mother. He asks a lot of different mothers (Mrs. Giraffe, Mrs. Penguin, Mrs. Walrus, and others) if he is their child. They point out the differences in their looks and he realizes that he does not belong to them. Choco never seems to match any of the animals. He finally asks Mrs. Bear and she lets him join her family, which is a mixture of all kinds of animals. Be sure to locate a copy of the actual story so that children can compare how close they came to predicting Kasza's story.

Miscellaneous Writing Prompts

Name _____ **Date** _____

Predict the Story!

1. little bird
2. wished
3. mother
4. find her
5. Mrs. Giraffe
6. Mrs. Penguin
7. Mrs. Walrus
8. couldn't find
9. Mrs. Bear
10. I could be
11. new mommy

_____
_____
_____
_____
_____
_____
_____
_____
_____
_____
_____
_____
_____
_____
_____

Describe Something in Unusual Terms

In the book *Seven Blind Mice,* by Ed Young, each mouse takes a turn trying to describe what it has touched. The mice are trying to describe an elephant. Since they are blind, they do not see that what they think is a snake is really a trunk. The spear is really a tusk. The pillar is really a leg and foot.

Have children imagine that they must describe something to a person who cannot see. Perhaps they will want to describe an elephant in their own terms. They also may choose another animal to describe. Tell them to pick an animal that reminds them of some object or objects, perhaps something that is human made, such as the spear and pillar in the story. Have children write a description of their animal that compares it to known objects.

Miscellaneous Writing Prompts

Name _____ **Date** _____

A_____ is like a _____ because . . .

Build a Circle Story

If You Give a Mouse a Cookie, If You Give a Moose a Muffin, and If You Give a Pig a Pancake, all written by Laura Numeroff, are books that contain series of events that revolve around unrelated items that cleverly come together to make a coherent story. The mouse, moose, and pig are given something that makes them think they need something else, which leads to the need for yet a different thing. The stories all manage to end where they began, with the cookie, the muffin, and the pancake.

Writing a true circle story (one where the end is the same as the beginning) is not easy. It should probably not be a requirement for this prompt. The creation of a story based upon a selection of unrelated items is a task in itself.

As an alternate exercise, have children compose stories in small groups. Arrange children in groups of three. Give each group a paper bag that contains six unrelated items. All bags should contain different items. Have each group write a story that mentions at least five of the six objects from their bag. Have them title their stories similar to Numeroff's titles.

Name _____ **Date** _____

If You Give a _____ a _____

A World of Sounds Around Us

There are sounds all around us. They might be the sounds of a train passing by or a marching band playing horns and drums. They might be the sounds of the animals on the farm or at the zoo. Brainstorm with children words that name sounds (onomatopoeia words—kids love to say that one!) and list on a chart.

Jim Aylesworth's *Country Crossing* is excellent for demonstrating how sound words help to tell a story. Changing voice intonation from loud to soft as you read will add interest to the story.

Ask children to select a place to listen to sounds and then write a description of sounds they hear. You might want to require that a minimum of three, four, five, or more onomatopoeias be used in their narratives.

As an alternative, let children listen to tapes of nature sounds. Sounds of the sea, whales, or a storm are just a few of those available. Have them write about the sounds they hear and how it makes them feel.

Name _____ **Date** _____

I listened to _____ and I heard . . .

_____

_____

_____

_____

_____

_____

_____

_____

_____

_____

_____

_____

_____

_____

_____

_____

_____

_____

_____

_____

_____

_____

_____

_____

Write Directions for Making Something

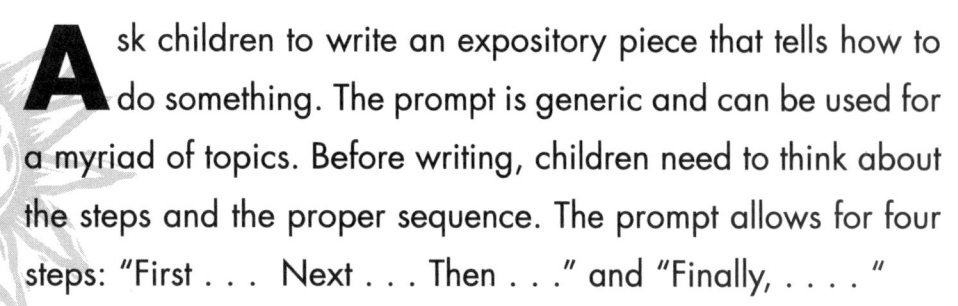

Ask children to write an expository piece that tells how to do something. The prompt is generic and can be used for a myriad of topics. Before writing, children need to think about the steps and the proper sequence. The prompt allows for four steps: "First . . . Next . . . Then . . ." and "Finally, ..."

Encourage children to select a simple "How to . . ." topic with a few steps rather than a complicated one. Sample simple topics include: washing the car, doing the dishes, cleaning a room, or making a bed.

Miscellaneous Writing Prompts

Name _____ **Date** _____

How to _____

First

_____

_____

_____

_____

Next

_____

_____

_____

_____

Then

_____

_____

_____

_____

Finally,

_____

_____

_____

_____

Add Text to a Wordless Picture Book

Tuesday, by David Wiesner, is a good example of a book that is virtually wordless. *Do You Want to Be My Friend?*, by Eric Carle, is another. Wiesner's book is quite complex; Carle's book is much more simple in its idea. Select a wordless picture book that matches the level of your students.

Share the pictures in the book. Talk about the possible story the pictures tell. If you are using a more complex book, allow groups of students to work together to write their stories. For timesaving purposes, you might assign each double page spread of a complex book to two or three students to caption. Then put all of the groups' works together for a complete story. If you assign separate pages in this way, make sure the class has a clear idea of the story to maintain continuity. There is no reproducible prompt for this writing idea.

As an alternate activity, Eric Carle's book noted above offers an opportunity to add speech bubbles above the character that is speaking. Cut sticky notes in the shape of speech bubbles, write dialogue on them, and place them in the correct spots in the book.

This activity is fun to do more than once during the school year. Look in your school library for a selection of wordless picture books. They are fun to pull off the shelf on a moment's notice!

Miscellaneous Writing Prompts   **353**

Guess My Animal

Mem Fox's *Hattie and the Fox* is a story about a fox who tries to sneak into the barnyard to capture something for lunch. Hattie, a hen, sees the fox and tries to let the other animals know that it is there. Hattie sees only a little bit of the fox at a time. She sees a nose, then eyes, ears, and the rest of the fox's body. No one realizes that she is describing a fox until it is almost too late!

Ask children to write clues that describe an animal. Make a guessing game out of this prompt. Have children share their clues aloud so that someone else can try to guess what they are describing.

Name _____ **Date** _____

Guess my animal!

An Alphabet Adventure

Jim Aylesworth's book, *Old Black Fly,* details the adventure of a fly as it buzzes around the house, bothering people and making messes wherever it goes. It is a unique and fun book because the adventure is written in alphabetical order, and with rhyme and rhythm. Children delight in joining in the reading by chanting the repetitive parts.

Ask children to write an adventure of an insect or animal as it makes its way through the house or school or neighborhood or other place of the writer's choosing. It would be an extremely difficult task for younger children to write a story using all twenty-six letters of the alphabet. Instead, let children select either six or twelve letters for their adventure. Depending upon the children's abilities, you can expect them to select letters in alphabetical order (example: j, k, l, m, n, o) or a random selection (example: b, f, h, m, p, t). Reproduce the following page in double sets if you decide on assigning twelve-letter stories.

Each box on the following page will be used for a letter and the words that tell the tale of the alphabet adventure. Select some of the stories and type them and put them together in book form, one letter per page. Let the children illustrate their adventures and share them with other children.

Name _____ Date _____

Letter ____

Letter ____

Letter ____

Letter ____

Letter ____

Letter ____

Guess My Friend

People come in all shapes and sizes. They have different skin colors, eye colors, and hair colors. Their noses, lips, and ears are different shapes and sizes as well. "Millions of People," a poem by Jane W. Krows (*Poetry Place Anthology*), helps readers to think about the differences we all have. Differences make each of us unique.

Have children describe a classmate by writing clues that will be shared aloud. Among the clues children might include are eye color, hair color, and perhaps skin color. The children also might describe clothing, favorite activities, or favorite books of the person they are describing. Allow for oral sharing of the descriptions to see if children can "guess who."

To be certain that every child gets described, have students draw names out of a hat. If anyone pulls out his or her own name, put it back and draw again!

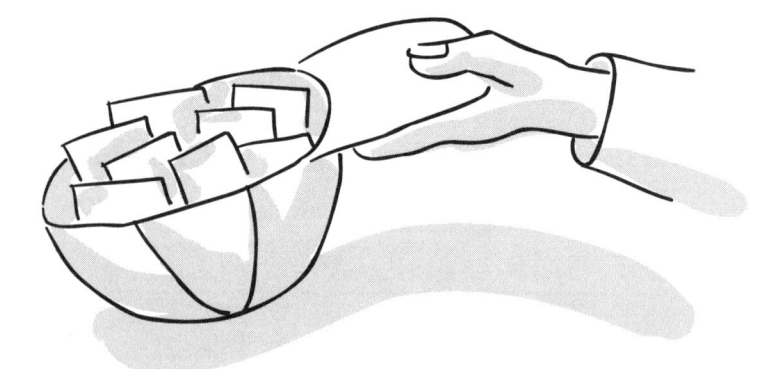

Miscellaneous Writing Prompts

Name _____ **Date** _____

Guess my friend!

A Letter to an Author

Children enjoy reading or listening to their favorite books time and time again. Personalize the event, if you can, by talking about the authors of their favorite books. Publications are available that provide background information on some of the more well-known authors.

Select an author for children to learn more about and to communicate with. Share what you can about the author. Discuss the information that they might include in a letter, such as naming their favorite book by that person, telling something about that author that was of interest to them personally, or giving suggestions for more book ideas. Then have children write a letter to that author.

Miscellaneous Writing Prompts

Dear _____ ,

_____
_____
_____
_____
_____
_____
_____
_____
_____
_____
_____
_____
_____
_____
_____
_____
_____
_____
_____

Your friend,

_____

Respond to a Particular Book or Poem

Select a book or poem that seems to relay a message or moral. Share the book or poem aloud. Stories such as *The Great Kapok Tree,* by Lynne Cherry, or *Thank You, Mr. Falker,* by Patricia Polacco, contain powerful messages. Ask children to write about what they think the message or moral of the story is.

Name _____ **Date** _____

The message in the story _____

by _____ is . . .

_____
_____
_____
_____
_____
_____
_____
_____
_____
_____
_____
_____
_____
_____
_____
_____
_____
_____
_____
_____
_____
_____
_____

Miscellaneous Writing Prompts

Use a Venn Diagram

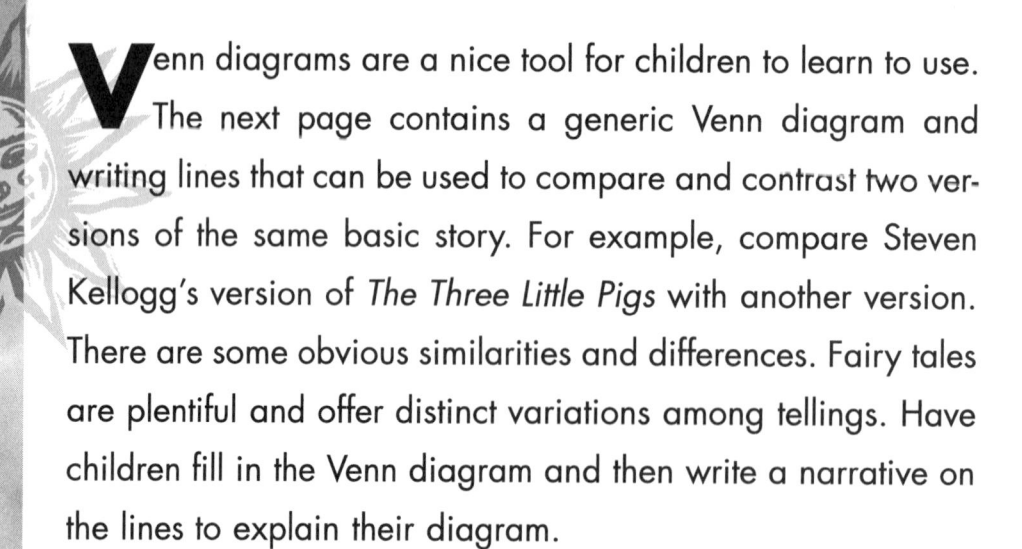

Venn diagrams are a nice tool for children to learn to use. The next page contains a generic Venn diagram and writing lines that can be used to compare and contrast two versions of the same basic story. For example, compare Steven Kellogg's version of *The Three Little Pigs* with another version. There are some obvious similarities and differences. Fairy tales are plentiful and offer distinct variations among tellings. Have children fill in the Venn diagram and then write a narrative on the lines to explain their diagram.

Name _____ **Date** _____

Miscellaneous Writing Prompts   **365**

Write a Tongue Twister

You can probably find a book in your library that contains some of the typical tongue twisters such as "Peter Piper picked a peck of pickled peppers." This writing prompt is based upon the tongue twister concept. The book *Four Famished Foxes and Fosdyke,* by Pamela Duncan Edwards, is a complete story filled with numerous words that begin with the letter *f*. A story is perhaps a bit harder to write than a simple tongue twister of a few sentences.

Have children select a single letter of the alphabet and write a story that contains many words that begin with that letter. Some stories will feel and sound like tongue twisters when they are read aloud. You might suggest that children choose their single letter and then brainstorm a list of words that begin with that letter before writing their actual stories.

You can use p. 368 for this writing prompt.

Find the Little Words

The book *Pets in Trumpets,* by Bernard Most, is filled with little words that can be found in bigger words. Choose a big word such as *hippopotamus*. Write it on the board or overhead projector. Set a timer for five minutes and ask children to use that time to make a list of at least six to ten little words that can be made from the letters in the big word.

When the timer signals the end of the five minutes, have children use the words they have written to create a story. The story should contain as many of the words in the list as possible.

Miscellaneous Writing Prompts

Name _____ **Date** _____

My Words

_____ _____ _____
_____ _____ _____
_____ _____ _____
_____ _____ _____

Here's my story!

Write a Parody About Jimmy's Boa

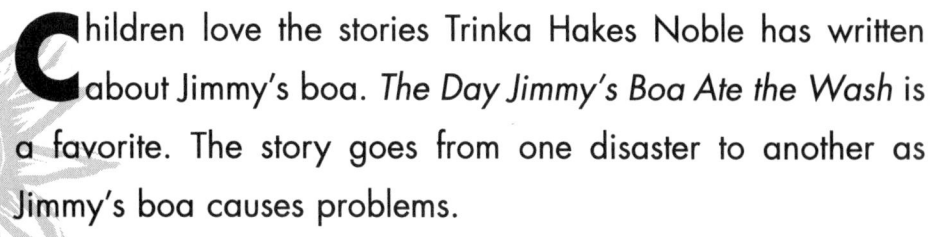

Children love the stories Trinka Hakes Noble has written about Jimmy's boa. *The Day Jimmy's Boa Ate the Wash* is a favorite. The story goes from one disaster to another as Jimmy's boa causes problems.

Ask children to think about some other problems that another animal might cause. Brainstorm a list of possibilities. Encourage them to use these ideas to help them write a parody. Examples of topics might be:

> The Day Jimmy's Pig Ate the Pizza
>
> The Day Jimmy's Cat Caught a Skunk
>
> The Day Jimmy's Parrot Swallowed a Whistle

Miscellaneous Writing Prompts

Name _____ **Date** _____

The day Jimmy's _____ . . .

Miscellaneous Writing Prompts

Write a Month-by-Month Story

A House for Hermit Crab, by Eric Carle, is a month-by-month tale about a hermit crab that adds things such as barnacles and anemones to its shell because it thinks its shell is too plain. This month-by-month story format can be parodied by using another subject.

Brainstorm with children and make a list of possible subjects for such a story format. Possible subjects include the development of a new baby brother or sister (from infancy to about 12–15 months of age), when a child learns to walk, the changes seen in a tree throughout the seasons, or the stages of building a structure, be it a house or a business.

You could also ask children to write a month-by-month story about themselves. This could be written near the end of the school year and might concentrate upon the months that school was in session for the current year. It would take on the format of diary entries written from hindsight.

Since there are two months on each page, you could reproduce the pages, cut them in half, and select only the months you need.

Name _____ **Date** _____

In January
_____
_____
_____
_____
_____
_____
_____
_____
_____

In February
_____
_____
_____
_____
_____
_____
_____
_____
_____

Miscellaneous Writing Prompts

Name _____ Date _____

In March

_____
_____
_____
_____
_____
_____
_____
_____
_____
_____

In April

_____
_____
_____
_____
_____
_____
_____
_____
_____
_____

Name _____ Date _____

In May

_____
_____
_____
_____
_____
_____
_____
_____
_____
_____

In June

_____
_____
_____
_____
_____
_____
_____
_____
_____
_____

Name _____ Date _____

In July

In August

Miscellaneous Writing Prompts

Name _____ **Date** _____

In September

_____
_____
_____
_____
_____
_____
_____
_____
_____

In October

_____
_____
_____
_____
_____
_____
_____
_____
_____

Name _____ **Date** _____

In November

_____
_____
_____
_____
_____
_____
_____
_____

In December

_____
_____
_____
_____
_____
_____
_____
_____
_____
_____

Miscellaneous Writing Prompts

Bibliography of Recommended Literature

Ahlberg, Allan. *Ten in a Bed.* Boston: Little, Brown and Company, ©1991.

Ahlberg, Janet and Ahlberg, Allan. *The Jolly Postman.* Boston: Little, Brown and Company, ©1991.

Ahlberg, Janet and Ahlberg, Allan. *The Jolly Christmas Postman, or, Other people's letters.* Boston: Little, Brown, ©1986.

Alexander, Rosemary, ed. *Poetry Place Anthology: More than 600 Poems for All Occasions.* New York: Instructor Publications, ©1983.

Asch, Frank. *Bear Shadow.* Englewood Cliffs, NJ: Prentice-Hall, ©1985.

Asch, Frank. *Milk and Cookies.* New York: Parents Magazine Press; Milwaukee: Gareth Stevens Pub., ©1992.

Asch, Frank. *Mooncake.* New York: Little Simon, [1988], ©1983.

Asch, Frank. *Pearl's Pirates.* New York: Delacorte Press, ©1987.

Asch, Frank. *Sand cake.* New York: Parents Magazine Press; Milwaukee: Gareth Stevens Publications, 1993.

Aylesworth, Jim. *Country Crossing/Clang, Clang, Clang*; illustrated by Ted Rand. New York: Atheneum; Toronto: Collier Macmillan Canada, 1991.

Aylesworth, Jim. *My Sister's Rusty Bike*; illustrated by Richard Hull. New York: Atheneum Books for Young Readers, 1996.

Aylesworth, Jim. *Old Black Fly*; illustrated by Stephen Gammell. New York: Holt, ©1992.

Aylesworth, Jim. *Teddy Bear Tears*; illustrated by Jo Ellen McAllister-Stammen. New York: Atheneum Books for Young Readers, ©1997.

Bagert, Brod. *Chicken Socks and Other Contagious Poems*; illustrations by Tim Ellis. Honesdale, PA.: Wordsong/Boyds Mills Press: Distributed by St. Martin's Press, 1993.

Bagert, Brod. *If Only I Could Fly: Poems for Kids to Read Out Loud*; illustrated by Stephen Morillo. New Orleans: Juliahouse, 1984.

Bagert, Brod. *Let Me be the Boss: Poems for Kids to Perform*; illustrated by G.L. Smith. Honesdale, PA.: Wordsong, 1992.

Barbour, Karen. *Little Nino's Pizzeria.* San Diego: Harcourt Brace Jovanovich, ©1987.

Baylor, Byrd. *Everybody Needs a Rock*; illustrated by Peter Parnall. New York: Atheneum, 1974.

Behn, Harry. *Trees*; illustrated by James Endicott. New York: H. Holt, ©1992.

Berends, Polly. *The Case of the Elevator Duck*; illustrated by Diane Allison. New York: Random House, 1989, ©1973.

Blume, Judy. *The Pain and the Great One/Free to be ... You and Me*; illustrated by Irene Trivas. Scarsdale, N.Y.: Bradbury Press, 1984, ©1974.

Brett, Jan. *The Mitten: A Ukrainian Folktale.* New York: Putnam, 1989.

Brown, Jeff. *Flat Stanley*; illustrated by Steve Björkman. New York: HarperTrophy, 1996.

Brown, Marc. *Arthur Goes to Camp.* Boston: Little, Brown, ©1982.

Brown, Marc. *Arthur Meets the President.* Boston: Joy Street Books, ©1991.

Brown, Marc. *Arthur's April Fool.* Boston: Joy Street Books, 1988.

Brown, Marc. *Arthur's Chicken Pox.* Boston: Little, Brown, ©1994.

Brown, Marc. *Arthur's Nose.* Boston: Little, Brown, ©1976.

Brown, Marc. *Arthur's Teacher Trouble.* Boston: Little, Brown, ©1986.

Brown, Marc. *Arthur's Tooth.* Boston: Atlantic Monthly Press, ©1985.

Brown, Ruth. *A Dark, Dark Tale.* New York: Dial Press, ©1981.

Browne, Anthony. *Piggybook.* New York: Knopf, ©1986.

Bruce, Lisa. *Oliver's Alphabets*; illustrated by Debi Gliori. New York: Bradbury Press; Toronto: Maxwell Macmillan Canada; New York: Maxwell Macmillan International, ©1993.

Bunting, Eve. *Secret Place*; illustrated by Ted Rand. New York: Clarion Books, ©1996.

Campbell, Rod. *Dear Zoo.* New York: Four Winds Press, 1983, ©1982.

Carle, Eric. *A House for Hermit Crab.* Saxonville, Mass.: Picture Book Studio, ©1987.

Carle, Eric. *Do You Want to be My Friend?* New York: Philomel Books, ©1988.

Carle, Eric. *The Grouchy Ladybug.* New York: HarperCollins, 1996.

Carle, Eric. *The Mixed-up Chameleon.* New York: Crowell, 1975.

Carle, Eric. *The Very Busy Spider.* New York: Philomel Books, ©1984.

Charlip, Remy. *Fortunately.* New York: Parents' Magazine Press 1964.

Cherry, Lynne. *The Armadillo From Amarillo.* San Diego: Harcourt Brace, ©1994.

Cherry, Lynne. *The Great Kapok Tree: A Tale of the Amazon Rain Forest.* San Diego: Harcourt Brace Jovanovich, ©1990.

Child, Lydia Maria. *Boy's Thanksgiving Day Over the River and Through the Wood: A Thanksgiving Poem*; illustrated with woodcuts by Christopher Manson. New York: North-South Books, ©1993.

Chwast, Seymour. *The Twelve Circus Rings.* San Diego: Harcourt Brace Jovanovich, ©1993.

Cole, Joanna. *The Magic School Bus Shows and Tells: A Book About Archaeology*; illustrated by Bruce Degen. New York: Scholastic, ©1997.

Cowley, Joy. *Little Brother's Haircut*; illustrated by Helen Humphries. Bothell WA.: Wright Group, 1998.

Cowley, Joy and Melser, June. *Mrs. Wishy-Washy*; illustrated by Elizabeth Fuller. Auckland, N.Z.: Shortland Publications, 1980.

Cuyler, Margery. *That's Good! That's Bad!* New York: H. Holt, ©1991.

dePaola, Tomie. *Little Grunt and the Big Egg: A Prehistoric Fairytale.* New York: Holiday House, ©1990.

Dubanevich, Arlene. *Pig William.* New York: Aladdin Books; London: Collier Macmillan, 1990, ©1985.

Edwards, Pamela Duncan. *Four Famished Foxes and Fosdyke*; illustrated by Henry Cole. New York: HarperCollins Publishers, ©1995.

Ehlert, Lois. *Red Leaf, Yellow Leaf.* San Diego: Harcourt Brace Jovanovich, ©1991.

Ehlert, Lois. *Snowballs.* San Diego: Harcourt Brace, ©1995.

Ehrlich, Amy, ed. *When I was Your Age: Original Stories About Growing Up.* Cambridge, Mass.: Candlewick Press, 1996.

Elias, Joyce. *Whose Toes are Those?*; illustrated by Cathy Sturm. Hauppauge, N.Y.: Barrons, 1992.

Farjeon, Eleanor. *Poems for Children.* Philadelphia: Lippincott, ©1951.

Fox, Mem. *Hattie and the Fox*; illustrated by Patricia Mullins. New York: Bradbury Press, 1988, ©1986.

Fox, Mem. *Tough Boris*; illustrated by Kathryn Brown. San Diego: Harcourt Brace Jovanovich, ©1994.

Galdone, Paul. *The Three Little Pigs.* New York: Clarion Books. 1970.

Gauch, Patricia Lee. *Christina Katerina & the Box*; Illustrated by Doris Burn. New York, Coward, McCann & Geoghegan, 1971.

Ginsburg, Mirra. *The Chick and the Duckling*; translated from the Russian of V. Suteyev, pictures by Jose & Ariane Aruego. London, Hamilton, 1973.

Gliori, Debi. *When I'm Big*. Cambridge, Mass.: Candlewick Press, 1994.

Grambling, Lois. *An Alligator Named...Alligator.* illustrated by Doug Cushman. New York: Barron's, ©1991.

Greene, Carol. *The Thirteen Days of Halloween*; illustrations by Tom Dunnington. Chicago: Childrens Press, ©1983.

Guilfoile, Elizabeth. *Nobody Listens to Andrew*; illustrated by Mary Stevens. Chicago, Follett Pub. Co., 1957.

Hague, Michael. *Teddy Bear, Teddy Bear: A Classic Action Rhyme.* illustrated by Michael Hague. New York: Morrow Junior Books, ©1993.

Heller, Ruth. *How to Hide a Crocodile and Other Reptiles*. New York: Grosset & Dunlap, ©1994.

Heller, Ruth. *How to Hide a Polar Bear and Other Mammals*. New York: Grosset and Dunlap, 1994.

Henkes, Kevin. *Lilly's Purple Plastic Purse*. New York: Greenwillow Books, ©1996.

Henkes, Kevin. *Owen*. New York: Greenwillow Books, ©1993

Hoban, Russell. *Bread and Jam for Frances*; pictures by Lillian Hoban. New York: HarperCollins, ©1993.

Hoff, Syd. *Danny and the Dinosaur*. New York: Harper Trophy, 1993.

Howe's, James. *I Wish I Were a Butterfly*. San Diego: Harcourt Brace Jovanovich, ©1987.

Hutchins, Pat. *Rosie's Walk*. New York: Macmillan, ©1968.

Hutchins, Pat. *The Wind Blew*. New York: Aladdin; Toronto: Maxwell Macmillan Canada; New York: Maxwell Macmillan International, 1993.

Hymes, Lucie and Hymes, James. *Hooray for Chocolate, and Other Easy-to-Read Jingles*. New York: W.R. Scott, 1960.

Jackson, Ellen. *Cinder Edna*; illustrated by Kevin O'Malley. New York: Lothrop, Lee & Shepard, ©1994.

Johnston, Tony. *Amber on the Mountain*. New York: Dial Books for Young Readers, ©1994.

Kasza, Keiko. *A Mother for Choco*. New York: Putnam, ©1992.

Keats, Ezra Jack. *The Snowy Day*. Harmondsworth. New York: Puffin Books, 1978, ©1962.

Kellogg, Steven. *The Three Little Pigs*; retold and illustrated by Steven Kellogg. New York: Morrow Junior Books, ©1997.

Kimmel, Eric. *Anansi & the Talking Melon*; illustrated by Janet Stevens. New York: Holiday House, ©1994.

Knowles, Sheena. *Edward the Emu*; illustrated by Rod Clement. Sydney: Collins Publishers Australia in association with A. Ingram Books, 1988 (1989 printing).

Kraus, Robert. *Leo the Late Bloomer*; pictures by Jose Aruego. New York: Windmill/Wanderer Books, 1980, ©1971.

Lamorisse, Albert. *Red Balloon*. Mankato, MN: Creative Education, ©1990.

Lester, Helen. *Listen Buddy*; illustrated by Lynn Munsinger. Boston: Houghton Mifflin, 1995.

Lester, Helen. *Tacky the Penguin*; illustrated by Lynn Munsinger. New York: Houghton Mifflin, 1988.

Lionni, Leo. *Frederick*. New York: Pantheon 1967.

MacLachlan, Patricia. *Through Grandpa's Eyes*; pictures by Deborah Ray. New York: Harper & Row, 1980.

Mahy, Margaret. *The Boy Who Was Followed Home*; pictures by Steven Kellogg. New York: F. Watts, 1975.

Marshall, Edward. *Four on the Shore*; pictures by James Marshall. New York: Dial Books for Young Readers, ©1985.

Marshall, James. *Fox on the Job*. New York: Dial Books for Young Readers, ©1988.

Martin, Jr., Bill. *Listen to the Rain*; illustrated by James Endicott. New York: H. Holt, ©1988.

Martin, Jr., Bill. *10 Little Caterpillars*; pictures by Gilbert Riswold. New York: Holt, Rinehart and Winston 1967.

Mayer, Mercer. *If I Had a Gorilla*; illustrated by Mercer Mayer. Inchelium, WA: Rain Bird Press, 1994.

Meddaugh, Susan. *Martha Speaks*. Boston: Houghton Mifflin, 1992.

Modesitt, Jeanne. *Sometimes I Feel Like a Mouse: A Book about Feelings*; illustrated by Robin Spowart. New York: Scholastic, 1992.

Most, Bernard. *If the Dinosaurs Came Back*. San Diego: Harcourt Brace, 1995.

Most, Bernard. *Pets in Trumpets*. San Diego: Harcourt Brace Jovanovich, ©1991.

Noble, Trinka Hakes. *The Day Jimmy's Boa Ate the Wash*; pictures by Steven Kellogg. New York: Dial Press, ©1980.

Numeroff, Laura. *If You Give a Moose a Muffin*; illustrated by Felicia Bond. New York: HarperCollins, ©1991.

Numeroff, Laura. *If You Give a Mouse a Cookie*; illustrated by Felicia Bond. New York: Harper & Row, ©1985.

Numeroff, Laura. *If You Give a Pig a Pancake*; illustrated by Felicia Bond. New York: Laura Geringer Book, 1998.

O'Hare, Jeff. *Searchin' Safari: Looking for Camouflaged Creatures*; illustrated by Marc Nadel. Honesdale, PA.: Bell Books; New York: Distributed by St. Martin's Press, 1992.

Pallotta, Jerry and Brian Cassie. *The Butterfly Alphabet Book*; illustrated by Mark Astrella. Watertown, MA: Charlesbridge, ©1995.

Pallotta, Jerry. *The Furry Alphabet Book*; illustrated by Edgar Stewart. Chicago: Childrens Press, 1991

Pallotta, Jerry. *The Icky Bug Counting Book*; title by Neil Pallotta; illustrated by Ralph Masiello. Watertown, Mass.: Charlesbridge, 1992.

Parkes, Brenda. *Who's in the Shed?*; illustrated by Ester Kasepuu. Melbourne, Australia: Maurbern Pty Ltd.; Crystal Lake, Illinois: Rigby Education, ©1986.

Pilkey, Dav. *Dogzilla: Starring Flash, Rabies, Dwayne, and introducing Leia as the Monster*. San Diego: Harcourt Brace Jovanovich, ©1993.

Pilkey, Dav. *Kat Kong: Starring Flash, Rabies, and Dwayne and introducing Blueberry as the Monster*. San Diego: Harcourt Brace Jovanovich, ©1993.

Pinkwater, Daniel. *The Big Orange Splot*. New York: Hastings House, ©1977.

Polacco, Patricia. *Thank You, Mr. Falker*. New York: Philomel Books, 1998.

Polacco, Patricia. *Thunder Cake*. New York: Philomel Books, ©1990

Pomerantz, Charlotte. *The Piggy in the Puddle*; pictures by James Marshall. New York: Aladdin Books, 1989, ©1974.

Potter, Beatrix. *The Tale of Peter Rabbit/Peter Rabbit*. Baltimore: Allan Publishers, ©1991.

Prelutsky, Jack. *The Random House Book of Poetry for Children*; illustrated by Arnold Lobel. New York: Random House, ©1983.

Rey, H.A. *Curious George Gets a Medal*; illustrated by H.A. Rey. Boston: Houghton Mifflin, 1957.

Rylant, Cynthia. *The Relatives Came*; illustrated by Stephen Gammell. New York: Bradbury Press, ©1985.

Schimmel, Schim. *Dear Children of the Earth: A Letter from Home*. Minocqua, WI: North Word Press, ©1994.

Scieszka, Jon. *The True Story of the Three Little Pigs*; as told to Jon Scieszka; illustrated by Lane Smith. New York, U.S.A.: Viking Kestrel, 1989.

Sendak, Maurice. *Seven Little Monsters*. New York: Harper & Row, ©1977.

Silverstein, Shel. *Where the Sidewalk Ends: The Poems and Drawings of Shel Silverstein*. New York: Harper and Row, 1974.

Sisulu, Elinor Batezat. *The Day Gogo Went to Vote: South Africa, April 1994*; illustrated by Sharon Wilson. Boston: Little, Brown, ©1996.

Small, David. *Imogene's Antlers*. New York: Crown Publishers, ©1985.

Snow, Alan. *How Dogs Really Work*. London: Collins, 1993.

Spinelli, Eileen. *Somebody Loves You, Mr. Hatch*; pictures by Paul Yalowitz. New York: Bradbury Press, ©1991.

Stevens, Janet. *Tops & Bottoms*; adapted and illustrated by Janet Stevens. San Diego: Harcourt Brace, ©1995.

Strete, Craig Kee. *They Thought They Saw Him*; pictures by Jose Aruego and Ariane Dewey. New York: Greenwillow Books, ©1996.

Thaler, Mike. *The Teacher from the Black Lagoon*; pictures by Jared Lee. New York: Scholastic, ©1989.

The Three Little Kittens. Pictures by T. Izawa and S. Hijikata. New York: Grosset and Dunlap, 1968.

Tolhurst, Marilyn. *Somebody and the Three Blairs*; illustrated by Simone Abel. New York: Orchard Books, 1991.

Tresselt, Alvin. *The Mitten: an Old Ukrainian Folktale/Rukavychka*; illustrated by Yaroslava; adapted from the version by E. Rachov. New York: Mulbery Books, 1989, ©1964.

Van Allsburg, Chris. *Two Bad Ants*. Boston: Houghton Mifflin, 1988.

Viorst, Judith. *Alexander, Who's Not (Do You Hear Me? I Mean It!) Going to Move*; illustrated by Robin Preiss-Glasser. New York: Atheneum Books for Young Readers, ©1995.

Waber, Bernard. *Ira Sleeps Over*. Boston, Houghton Mifflin, 1972.

Ward, Cindy. *Cookie's Week*; illustrated by Tomie dePaola. New York: Putnam, ©1988.

Watson, Joy. *Grandpa's Slippers*; illustrated by Wendy Hodder. Auckland; N.Y.: Ashton Scholastic, 1989.

Watson, Pauline. *Wriggles the Little Wishing Pig*; pictures by Paul Galdone. New York: Seabury Press, ©1978.

Wells, Rosemary. *McDuff Moves In*; pictures by Susan Jeffers. New York: Hyperion Books for Children, ©1997.

Wiesner, David. *Tuesday*. New York: Clarion Books, ©1991.

Williams, Rebel. *The Nine Days of Camping*; illustrated by Dennis Hockerman. Bothell, WA.: Wright Group, 1990.

Williams, Sue. *I Went Walking*; illustrated by Julie Vivas. San Diego: Harcourt Brace, 1996.

Wood, Audrey. *Heckedy Peg*; illustrated by Don Wood. San Diego: Harcourt Brace Jovanovich, ©1987.

Wood, Audrey. *Quick As a Cricket*; illustrated by Don Wood. New York, New York: Child's Play (International), 1990.

Wood, Audrey. *Silly Sally*. San Diego: Harcourt Brace Jovanovich, ©1992.

Wu, Norbert. *Fish Faces*. New York: Holt, ©1993.

Young, Ed. *Seven Blind Mice/Blind Men and the Elephant*. New York: Philomel Books, ©1992.

Zemach, Margot. *The Three Wishes: An Old Story*. New York: Farrar, Straus and Giroux, 1986.